SpringerBriefs in Education

We are delighted to announce SpringerBriefs in Education, an innovative product type that combines elements of both journals and books. Briefs present concise summaries of cutting-edge research and practical applications in education. Featuring compact volumes of 50 to 125 pages, the SpringerBriefs in Education allow authors to present their ideas and readers to absorb them with a minimal time investment. Briefs are published as part of Springer's eBook Collection. In addition, Briefs are available for individual print and electronic purchase.

SpringerBriefs in Education cover a broad range of educational fields such as: Science Education, Higher Education, Educational Psychology, Assessment & Evaluation, Language Education, Mathematics Education, Educational Technology, Medical Education and Educational Policy.

SpringerBriefs typically offer an outlet for:

- An introduction to a (sub)field in education summarizing and giving an overview of theories, issues, core concepts and/or key literature in a particular field
- A timely report of state-of-the art analytical techniques and instruments in the field of educational research
- A presentation of core educational concepts
- An overview of a testing and evaluation method
- A snapshot of a hot or emerging topic or policy change
- An in-depth case study
- A literature review
- A report/review study of a survey
- An elaborated thesis

Both solicited and unsolicited manuscripts are considered for publication in the SpringerBriefs in Education series. Potential authors are warmly invited to complete and submit the Briefs Author Proposal form. All projects will be submitted to editorial review by editorial advisors.

SpringerBriefs are characterized by expedited production schedules with the aim for publication 8 to 12 weeks after acceptance and fast, global electronic dissemination through our online platform SpringerLink. The standard concise author contracts guarantee that:

- an individual ISBN is assigned to each manuscript
- each manuscript is copyrighted in the name of the author
- the author retains the right to post the pre-publication version on his/her website or that of his/her institution

Peter Anderson · Levon Blue · Thu Pham ·
Melanie Saward

Higher Degree by Research

Factors for Indigenous Student Success

Springer

Peter Anderson ⓘ
Carumba Institute
Queensland University of Technology
Kelvin Grove, QLD, Australia

Levon Blue ⓘ
Carumba Institute
Queensland University of Technology
Kelvin Grove, QLD, Australia

Thu Pham ⓘ
Carumba Institute
Queensland University of Technology
Kelvin Grove, QLD, Australia

Melanie Saward ⓘ
Carumba Institute
Queensland University of Technology
Kelvin Grove, QLD, Australia

ISSN 2211-1921　　　　　　　ISSN 2211-193X　(electronic)
SpringerBriefs in Education
ISBN 978-981-19-5177-0　　　ISBN 978-981-19-5178-7　(eBook)
https://doi.org/10.1007/978-981-19-5178-7

© The Author(s) 2022. This book is an open access publication.
Open Access This book is licensed under the terms of the Creative Commons Attribution 4.0 International License (http://creativecommons.org/licenses/by/4.0/), which permits use, sharing, adaptation, distribution and reproduction in any medium or format, as long as you give appropriate credit to the original author(s) and the source, provide a link to the Creative Commons license and indicate if changes were made.
The images or other third party material in this book are included in the book's Creative Commons license, unless indicated otherwise in a credit line to the material. If material is not included in the book's Creative Commons license and your intended use is not permitted by statutory regulation or exceeds the permitted use, you will need to obtain permission directly from the copyright holder.
The use of general descriptive names, registered names, trademarks, service marks, etc. in this publication does not imply, even in the absence of a specific statement, that such names are exempt from the relevant protective laws and regulations and therefore free for general use.
The publisher, the authors, and the editors are safe to assume that the advice and information in this book are believed to be true and accurate at the date of publication. Neither the publisher nor the authors or the editors give a warranty, expressed or implied, with respect to the material contained herein or for any errors or omissions that may have been made. The publisher remains neutral with regard to jurisdictional claims in published maps and institutional affiliations.

This Springer imprint is published by the registered company Springer Nature Singapore Pte Ltd.
The registered company address is: 152 Beach Road, #21-01/04 Gateway East, Singapore 189721, Singapore

Acknowledgments

We would like to acknowledge the support provided to the National Indigenous Research and Knowledges Network (NIRAKN) from the Australian Research Council through the Special Research Initiative grant SR120100005. This funding made it possible to conduct capacity-building workshops with Indigenous higher degree by research (HDR) students and research and write this book. The comments from the three anonymous reviewers who considered this proposal and the reviewers who read the completed manuscript provided additional feedback that helped to shape this book. Thank you to all the Indigenous HDR students across Australia who attended NIRAKN capacity-building workshops and/or completed surveys and/or interviews.

Contents

1 **Indigenous Peoples and Higher Degrees by Research in Higher Education** 1
   1.1 Background 1
   1.2 Aims of This Book and Research Questions 4
   1.3 Overview of This Book 5
   1.4 Reciprocity, Respect, Equality, Responsibility, Survival and Protection, Spirit and Integrity 8
   References 9

2 **Academic Practices: Current Strategies to Attract and Retain Indigenous Higher Degree by Research Students in Australia** 11
   2.1 Introduction 11
   2.2 The Participation and Retention of Indigenous Students in Australian Higher Education 12
   2.3 Indigenous HDR Students' Barriers in Higher Education 15
      2.3.1 Lack of Academic and Research Skill Set 15
      2.3.2 Lack of Academic Support 16
      2.3.3 Issues in the Student–Supervisor Relationship 17
      2.3.4 Issues Related to Health, Family, Community Responsibilities and Financial Hardship 19
   2.4 Current Academic Practices to Support Indigenous HDR Students 20
   2.5 Summary 22
   References 23

3 **Capacity-Building Support for Indigenous HDR Students via the National Indigenous Research and Knowledges Network** 27
   3.1 Introduction 27
   3.2 Methodology and Data Analysis 29
   3.3 The Workshops 29
   3.4 Networking 31
   3.5 Do I Belong? 32

	3.6	Realising I Do Belong	32
	3.7	Learning How to Play 'The Game'	33
	3.8	Becoming an Academic	34
		3.8.1 Confirmation	34
		3.8.2 Data Collection	34
		3.8.3 Data Analysis	35
		3.8.4 Write Up	35
		3.8.5 Presentations	36
	3.9	The Legacy Phase	36
	References		37
4	**The Role of Agency in Higher Education: Acquiring Academic Capital**		**39**
	4.1	Introduction	39
	4.2	Identity, Agency, Culture and Capital	40
	4.3	Participants, Data Collection and Analysis	42
	4.4	Instances When Agency in a Higher Education Context Might Be Needed	44
		4.4.1 The Role of Agency Navigating the Terrain of Academia as an Indigenous HDR Student	44
		4.4.2 The Role of Agency When Indigenous HDR Students Encounter Racism in Higher Education Settings	45
		4.4.3 The Role of Agency When the Relationship Between the Indigenous HDR Student and the Supervisor Fails	47
		4.4.4 The Role of Agency When Indigenous HDR Students Need to Reach Out for Additional Academic Support	47
	4.5	Summary	48
	References		48
5	**Indigenous Higher Degree by Research Students' Needs and Experiences**		**51**
	5.1	Introduction	51
	5.2	Background	52
	5.3	Quality Supervision	52
	5.4	Supervising Indigenous HDR Students	53
	5.5	Participants	54
		5.5.1 Data Collection	54
		5.5.2 Data Analysis on Indigenous HDR Students' Needs and Experiences of Research Supervision	54
	5.6	What We Need	56
		5.6.1 Students Need Quality Supervision	56
		5.6.2 Supervisors with Expertise and Experience	58

		5.6.3 Mentoring Opportunities	60
		5.6.4 Access to Research Training	61
	5.7	Summary	63
	References		63
6	**The Needs and Experiences of Supervisors of Indigenous Higher Degree by Research Students**		67
	6.1	Introduction	67
		6.1.1 Supervising Indigenous HDR Students	68
		6.1.2 Roles and Responsibilities of Supervisors	69
	6.2	Methodology	70
	6.3	Results	71
		6.3.1 Demographic Questions	71
		6.3.2 Quality Supervision from Supervisors' Perspectives	72
		6.3.3 Good Practices and Concerns in Supervising HDR Students	77
		6.3.4 Professional Development for Supervisors of Indigenous HDR Students	83
	6.4	Discussion	85
		6.4.1 Supervisors of Indigenous HDR Students' Experiences: Quality Supervision	86
		6.4.2 Supervisors of Indigenous HDR Students' Needs: Professional Development	87
	6.5	Summary	88
	References		89
7	**Undoing Commonly Held Beliefs About Indigenous HDR Students**		91
	7.1	Introduction	91
	7.2	Data Used to Inform This Chapter	92
	7.3	Myth One: Indigenous HDR Students Need to Be Supervised by Indigenous Supervisor	93
	7.4	Myth Two: Indigenous HDR Students Need to Use Indigenous Research Methodologies	97
		7.4.1 Indigenous Research Methodologies	97
		7.4.2 Indigenous Research Methodologies: Use Is Not Compulsory	99
	7.5	Myth Three: Indigenous HDR Students Should Be Researching Indigenous Issues	101
	7.6	Summary	102
	References		102
8	**What We Need for Success: Recommendations and Wishes**		105
	8.1	Overview	105
	8.2	Data Used to Inform This Chapter	106
	8.3	Recommendations for Higher Education Institutions	107

8.4	Recommendations for Supervisors	108
8.5	Students' Suggestions for Improved Supervision	108
8.6	Recommendations for Prospective Indigenous HDR Students	110
8.7	Summary	111
References		112

About the Authors

Prof. Peter Anderson is from the Walpiri and Murinpatha First Nations in the Northern Territory. His research theorises the understandings of the organisational value of academic freedom in Australian universities and also more broadly in the polar south. His research areas include organisational leadership, Indigenous peoples' education and teacher and academic professional development. His research has been funded through Office of Learning and Teaching (OLT) grants. One grant investigated the improvement of initial teacher education providers' capacity to prepare preservice teachers to be confident, competent and culturally responsive to work in remote locations with high Indigenous populations. The second grant examined how to best engage and partner with Aboriginal and Torres Strait Islander parents and community to improve student outcomes. He is also lead Chief Investigator on an Australian Research Council (ARC)-funded Special Research Initiative (SRI) titled 'National Indigenous Research and Knowledges Network' (NIRAKN). He has just completed a research project that explored the needs and experiences of Indigenous HDR students and supervisors.

Dr. Levon Blue (Nimki Nibi Kwe) is Anishinaabe kwe (woman) who is a member of the Beausoleil First Nations (G'Chimnissing) who is originally from Canada and lives on Turrbal and Yugara country in Queensland, Australia. She is a senior lecturer and National Indigenous Research and Knowledges Network (NIRAKN) coordinator at the Carumba Institute at the Queensland University of Technology (QUT). She also holds an adjunct research professor position at Western University (Canada). She works with Indigenous peoples in both Australia and Canada on Community-driven research projects, including the financial literacy needs related to First Nations' trust accounts, small business owners and the needs and experiences of Indigenous HDR students. She is Chief Investigator on two Australian Research Council-funded grants: Special Research Initiative—National Indigenous Research and Knowledges Network (NIRAKN) and Discovery Indigenous—Empowering Indigenous Businesses Through Improved Financial and Commercial Literacy. She is currently working on three other research projects regarding the role of education and technology in First Nation Trust Settlements; how young adults interact with digital financial tools; and developing financially capable citizens in an era of finance apps and cryptocurrencies.

Dr. Thu Pham currently works as Research Project Officer at the Carumba Institute, QUT. She completed her doctoral degree in Education at QUT, Australia, in 2016. Her doctoral research study focused on leadership to support quality improvement in Vietnamese higher education. Her research interests are leadership in higher education and higher education reforms in Asia-Pacific countries. Recently, she has worked on Indigenous education and support for Indigenous HDR students' projects.

Melanie Saward is a proud descendant of the Wakka Wakka and Bigambul peoples. She is an associate lecturer of creative writing in the School of Creative Practice at QUT and a Ph.D. candidate.

Abbreviations

ARC	Australian Research Council
CI	Chief Investigator
HDR	Higher degree by research
IPSO	Indigenous Postgraduate Support Officer
ISU	Indigenous Support Unit
NIRAKN	National Indigenous Research and Knowledges Network
SRI	Special Research Initiative

List of Tables

Table 1.1	Datasets from 2018 to 2021	3
Table 3.1	Datasets relating to NIRAKN	30
Table 4.1	Datasets used to inform this chapter	43
Table 5.1	Datasets used to inform this chapter	55
Table 6.1	Dataset used to inform this chapter	70
Table 7.1	Datasets used to inform this chapter	94
Table 8.1	Dataset used to inform this chapter	107

Chapter 1
Indigenous Peoples and Higher Degrees by Research in Higher Education

Abstract This chapter provides an overview of the research conducted about the needs and experiences of Indigenous higher degree by research (HDR) students. We conducted multiple studies (six datasets in total) that included evaluation forms from capacity-building workshops, group discussions, written responses, online surveys to Indigenous HDR students ($n = 114$) and supervisors of Indigenous HDR students ($n = 33$) focusing on their needs and experiences and an evaluation survey of a national program. Of the six datasets, all but one are from Indigenous HDR students. All of these sources of data collected have helped to inform this book. We argue that Indigenous peoples are not the problem that need 'fixing' to increase HDR completions rates; rather, the system needs addressing to better support Indigenous HDR students. This book is written to privilege the voices of the Indigenous HDR students who were involved in this research. Through the chapters, we will undo and/or dispel some misunderstandings that continue to persist in higher education institutions about what Indigenous HDR students need to succeed in the academy. We challenge these assumptions using the insights shared by Indigenous HDR students who told us about their needs and experiences in higher education. This chapter provides the background, states the aims of the book and the research question guiding this study and provides an overview of each chapter in this book. We have written this book for anyone interested in successful pathways for Indigenous HDR students.

Keywords Indigenous · Higher education · Success · Support · NIRAKN · Capacity building

1.1 Background

The number of Aboriginal and Torres Strait Islander peoples (hereafter referred to as Indigenous peoples) enrolling in higher degree by research (HDR) has increased over the last decade. Unfortunately, the completion rates of Indigenous HDRs have remained relatively low (Moreton-Robinson et al., 2020). A range of factors continue to affect the retention and completion rates of Indigenous HDR students, including access to high-quality research supervision (Behrendt et al., 2012; Raciti et al., 2018;

Schofield et al., 2013; Trudgett, 2013, 2014), racism, discrimination and low socio-economic status (Hutchings et al., 2018, 2019; Schofield et al., 2013). Similar retention and completion rates issues affecting Indigenous HDR students are occurring in other countries, including Canada (Childs et al., 2016) and New Zealand (Schofield et al., 2013; Wilson et al., 2011). One reason for low completion rates by Indigenous HDR students relates to insufficient Indigenous methodological and cultural knowledge from their supervisors (Grant & McKinley, 2011). As such, Hutchings et al. (2019) identified supervisor knowledge and training as a success factor for Indigenous peoples in higher education.

Quality supervision is key to Indigenous HDR students' success and a primary concern of most HDR students (Trudgett, 2011). Many studies have identified contributing factors to 'quality' supervision of Indigenous HDR students (Laycock et al., 2009; Pihama et al., 2019; Schofield et al., 2013; Trudgett, 2011, 2013, 2014). These include supervisors' mentoring expertise, availability and respect for students and readiness to provide students with culturally specific support, as well as compatibility within the supervisory team. The need for quality cross-cultural supervision due to insufficient experienced Indigenous supervisors was also identified (Wilson et al., 2017). While our research shares some parallels with these studies, it provides insight from Indigenous HDR students on supervision practices in an Australian context and may be of relevance for other countries.

Previous studies have relied primarily on quantitative data, which may limit the depth of responses. We report on the findings from our mostly qualitative studies but include three surveys that collected quantitative demographic information with open-ended responses that were conducted with Indigenous HDR students from different academic disciplines who were enrolled in higher education institutions across Australia and/or were supervisors of Indigenous HDR students. In total, six types of data were collected and analysed for this research, as shown in Table 1.1.

We will now discuss the above datasets in more detail and point to the chapters that will use this data. In Chap. 3, datasets 1 and 2 are used when discussing the capacity-building workshops run by the National Indigenous Research and Knowledges Network (NIRAKN). Dataset 1 included all of the NIRAKN capacity-building workshops that took place in 2018, which included one 5-day beginners capacity-building workshop, 1 two-day Indigenous research methodology master class, 1 one-day critical writing workshop facilitated by the National State Hub Leader and Director of NIRAKN, Professor Peter Anderson and Dr. Levon Blue (NIRAKN coordinator). Dr. David Singh and Distinguished Professor Aileen Moreton-Robinson also facilitated the 5-day Beginners Capacity Building Workshop. In 2018, a one-day workshop that covered a bit of everything was presented by all of the State Hub Leaders of NIRAKN and Distinguished Professor Moreton-Robinson. Dataset 2 was administered online and consisted of an online survey seeking the views of past NIRAKN participants about the capacity-building workshops that were offered. The feedback received was in the form of qualitative responses.

Chapter 4 explores the role of agency in a higher education context. The datasets used to inform this chapter included datasets 3, 4, 5 and 6, which included written evaluation forms, online surveys and written responses. Chapter 5 focuses on the

1.1 Background

Table 1.1 Datasets from 2018 to 2021

Dataset number	Type (written evaluation form, group discussion, written response and/or online survey)	Year collected	What it is and who it includes	Number of participants	Referred to in text as
1	Written evaluation form (qualitative)	2018	NIRAKN workshop evaluations (Indigenous HDR students)	65	WEF_IndigenousHDR#
2	Online survey (qualitative with quantitative demographic information)	2021	NIRAKN evaluation (former Indigenous HDR students)	13	OLS1_IndigenousHDR#
3	Group discussion (qualitative)	2018	Discussion about needs and experiences of Indigenous HDRs (Indigenous HDR students)	34	GD_IndigenousHDR
4	Individual written responses (qualitative)	2018	Written responses about needs and experiences of Indigenous HDR students (Indigenous HDR students)	34[a]	IWR_IndigenousHDR#
5	Online survey (qualitative and quantitative demographic information)	2020	Survey about the needs and experiences of Indigenous HDR students (Indigenous HDR students)	32	OLS2_IndigenousHDR#
6	Online survey (qualitative and quantitative demographic information)	2020	Survey about the needs and experiences of Indigenous HDR students (supervisors and Indigenous HDR students)	33	OLS3_Supervisor#
Total participants				147	

[a] The same participants who completed the group discussion also provided a written response to additional questions. We only counted these participants once despite it being two different sets of data

needs and experiences of Indigenous HDR students. Datasets 3, 4 and 5 were used to inform this chapter, including audio-recorded group discussions, written responses to questions and an online survey. Chapter 6 focuses on the views of supervisors of Indigenous HDR students (dataset 6); however, datasets 3 and 4 are also used to compare and contrast what Indigenous HDR students are also reporting about these themes. Chapter 7 is the last chapter before our recommendations, in which datasets 3, 4, 5 and 6 are used to inform its findings. This chapter focuses on identifying some commonly held myths about Indigenous HDR students and challenging the myths with insights from Indigenous HDR students who report what they 'actually' need for success. Chapter 8 builds on previous recommendations that were informed by datasets 3 and 4 by analysing and reporting on findings from dataset 5.

In Chaps. 3–7, we identify the datasets used and describe the data analysis process used to thematically analyse and identify the needs and experiences of both Indigenous HDR students and supervisors of Indigenous HDR students. Throughout these chapters, we reveal disparities between HDR students' expectations (wants) and their actual needs and how these are fulfilled and/or unfulfilled by their supervisory team. We found there was a disconnect between the students' understanding of the supervisory process as opposed to the institutional requirements of supervision and that there were commonly held beliefs about Indigenous HDR students, such as the beliefs that they need to be researching Indigenous issues, that they need to be supervised by Indigenous supervisors and that they need to use Indigenous research methodologies. We unpack these assumptions or 'myths' and share what Indigenous HDRs report they need to experience success in higher education.

Respectful relationships, discipline knowledge from their supervisors and opportunities to build their CV during candidature were identified as key factors in a successful HDR experience. We also share the experiences from supervisors of Indigenous HDR students and report what further opportunities exist to enhance the higher education experiences of Indigenous HDR students. We then identify how successful relationships between Indigenous HDR students and their supervisors may be fostered.

Last, despite focusing on Indigenous HDR students in an Australian higher education context, this book may be a valuable resource for Indigenous peoples wishing to pursue higher education in countries with Indigenous populations, as well as for supervisors of HDR students in those countries.

1.2 Aims of This Book and Research Questions

The main aim of this book is to privilege the voices of Indigenous HDR students who have shared their needs and experiences in academia. From the insights shared, we aim to identify successful pathways in higher education institutions as informed by Indigenous HDR students. Our research is informed by datasets 1 through 6, which also involved some of the authors' experiences in facilitating NIRAKN capacity-building workshops (Professor Peter Anderson and Dr. Levon Blue) and one author

(Melanie Saward) who participated in NIRAKN workshops during her HDR. Based on our experience, we can report that assumptions about what Indigenous HDR students need are often viewed as homogenous. For instance, we were told by non-Indigenous academics that Indigenous HDR students need to use Indigenous research methodologies when conducting research; or that Indigenous HDR students need to be supervised by Indigenous academics rather than an academic with relevant discipline expertise. We were also informed that Indigenous HDR students are assumed to focus on a research topic related to Indigenous issues. We wonder how these three assumptions about Indigenous HDR students impact their 'choice' and 'success' in academia. Choice discourses reinforce hegemonic power structures by pathologising individuals, by ignoring the role of power and social structures (Pinto & Coulson, 2011). So, although we understand the dangers of assuming individuals have 'choice' beyond the power and social structures within higher education for Indigenous HDR students, their perceived 'choice' may be further limited by assumptions made about what they *ought* to be doing. By 'success', what this means to Indigenous HDR students likely might not be the same thing (O'Shea & Delahunty, 2019), but for the purposes of this book, 'success' is connected to completion of the research degree. Although we did not ask Indigenous HDR students what 'success' means in a higher education context, throughout this book, we share insights from Indigenous HDR students that were collected from 2018 to 2021 (as shown in Table 1.1—datasets 1–6).

As such, the *research questions* guiding this book are:

(1) How are Indigenous HDR students enabled to succeed?
(2) What are the experiences and needs of Indigenous HDR students?
(3) What additional support is required to ensure Indigenous HDR students complete their research degrees?
(4) What professional development is required for supervisors of Indigenous HDR students to enable students to complete their HDR degrees?

We sought to understand from Indigenous HDR students what they believe is needed to succeed instead of what can be seen as assumptions by the academy. We obtained these insights after delivering capacity-building workshops, via group discussions, written responses and/or online surveys. We also asked supervisors of Indigenous HDR students ($n = 34$) for insights about what they believe is needed when supervising an Indigenous HDR candidate through to completion. However, the majority of responses ($n = 147$) came from Indigenous HDR students. Next, we provide an overview of this book by providing an overview of each of the eight chapters.

1.3 Overview of This Book

This book contains eight chapters, including this introductory chapter, which provides an overview of the context of the research and the data we collected. This introductory chapter will set the scene by identifying what is happening in the higher education space for Indigenous HDR students, what capacity building we have been involved in and where more work is needed based on the findings from our research.

Chapter 2 provides an overview of barriers and supports relating to Indigenous HDR students by exploring the literature about Australian higher education institutions and international higher education institutions. The number of Indigenous HDR students has increased steadily over the past decade. Support for Indigenous students from the Australian government, universities and Indigenous Support Units has been documented in Australian higher education. Unfortunately, a range of barriers continue to hinder Indigenous HDR students' completion of their degrees in their research journey. This chapter provides a literature review of those barriers, which include the lack of academic skill sets and research skills to pursue a research degree program, lack of social and academic support for Indigenous HDR students, the student–supervisor relationship issues and challenges relating to health, family and community responsibilities. Simultaneously, our review identified current strategies and initiatives to retain Indigenous HDR students in their research degree programs and to support them to completion, highlighting the roles of the Indigenous Postgraduate Support Officer and NIRAKN. This review, we suggest, should move further to analyse the effectiveness of current strategies and initiatives provided for Indigenous HDR students in detail to inform Indigenous students of the available support resources and how to access to these resources.

In Chap. 3, we describe the capacity-building workshops that Indigenous HDR students have had an opportunity to participate in via NIRAKN. The workshops covered basic information about completing a research degree, including how to navigate academia, how to read and write critically and an introduction to Indigenous research methodologies. In this chapter, an overview of what NIRAKN set out to achieve and what has been accomplished is discussed. Evaluation forms completed by Indigenous HDR students who attended capacity-building workshops were analysed to understand what students found to be beneficial when participating in NIRAKN events. Here, we share the findings and offer insights into ways higher education institutions can support Indigenous HDR students in the successful completion of their degrees.

In Chap. 4, we discuss the role of agency in higher education. We argue that Indigenous HDR students navigating higher education institutions continue to face additional challenges that are not associated with the research degree they are pursuing. Racism continues to be identified as a barrier in academic settings and society. The impact of racism may affect an individual's agency and their ability to acquire academic capital. Both agency and academic capital may also influence how an individual is supported throughout their candidature and ultimately become a factor in the success of the HDR students' research degree. In this chapter, we discuss the role of agency and academic capital among Indigenous HDR students and then connect our findings about how Indigenous HDR students report that agency and/or academic capital has influenced their experience in higher education.

1.3 Overview of This Book

Chapter 5 focuses on the Indigenous HDR students' needs and experiences in academia. The study employed qualitative research methods including group discussions and individual written responses ($n = 34$) and an online survey ($n = 32$). The participants were Indigenous HDR students from different disciplinary fields from across Australia who participated in this research during 2018 and 2020. Specifically, this research project explored the students' needs and experiences during their candidature. We found that the role of supervisors in the students' HDR journey impacted their sense of agency and opportunities for mentorship and networking within their discipline. Indigenous HDR students specifically reported the need for: (1) quality supervision; (2) mentoring opportunities; and (3) access to research training. The reported needs bring the spotlight on how increasing retention rates of Indigenous HDR students might be possible.

Chapter 6 focuses on supervision as an influence of HDR students' success, as well as the key role supervisors play in triggering these students' capabilities. Furthermore, quality supervision provided to Indigenous HDR students has recently attracted the interest of many researchers in this field. This chapter provides an overview of the needs and experiences of supervisors of Indigenous HDR students. We surveyed 33 supervisors to understand their needs and experiences when supervising Indigenous HDR candidates. The perceptions of quality supervision, the good practices and concerns of supervisors and the professional development required for supervising Indigenous HDR students were asked of supervisors who participated in our study. Our study found that it is the mental health and well-being of Indigenous HDR students that raises concerns with their supervisors, while racism is still seen as prevalent. Keeping Indigenous HDR students motivated and on track and supporting Indigenous HDR students physically, mentally and academically were found to be significant concerns for supervisors.

Chapter 7 highlights the commonly held beliefs about Indigenous HDR students and offers ways to reframe these beliefs. This chapter draws on our experience in facilitating the NIRAKN capacity-building workshops. During these workshops, we continually heard what we refer to as 'the three myths about what an Indigenous HDR student ought to be doing'. The three myths are that an Indigenous HDR student needs to be: (1) supervised by an Indigenous supervisor, (2) using Indigenous research methodologies and (3) researching Indigenous issues. Following these workshops, we sought to understand the needs and experience of Indigenous HDR students and also the supervisors of these students. Informing this chapter are group discussions, written responses and surveys conducted with Indigenous HDR students ($n = 66$) and supervisors ($n = 33$). In this chapter, we argue against these myths to demonstrate that discipline expertise and/or methodological expertise is the most important variable that determines how all HDR students are paired with supervisors. We also argue that it is harmful and racist to expect Indigenous HDR students to use a prescribed methodology that is race-based. And that, the assumption that Indigenous HDR students should be researching Indigenous matters rather than their own research interests is problematic.

In Chap. 8, we conclude the book by synthesising what is needed for Indigenous HDR success. Throughout this book, we shared our experiences in conducting capacity-building workshops and undertaking research about the needs and experiences of Indigenous HDR students in Australia. In total, we heard from 147 participants, which included 113 Indigenous HDR students from across Australia and 34 supervisors of Indigenous HDR students. The insights received from both the students and supervisors revealed that there are still opportunities to improve the HDR experience for Indigenous students. Based on our findings, in this chapter, we expand on the recommendations outlined in the Moreton-Robinson et al.'s (2020) report to include new data collected in 2020 from 32 Indigenous HDR students. We hope our recommendations, once acted upon, will have a positive impact on the success of Indigenous HDRs and that the insights shared by the Indigenous HDR candidates we heard from will have meaning and relevance for anyone pursuing a research degree.

Next, we discuss what guided the research project undertaken with Indigenous HDR students and/or supervisors of Indigenous HDRs students.

1.4 Reciprocity, Respect, Equality, Responsibility, Survival and Protection, Spirit and Integrity

The values of reciprocity, respect, equality, responsibility, survival and protection, spirit and integrity (National Health and Medical Research Council [NHMRC], 2018) have shaped our practices and guided our approach.

In this project, we demonstrate spirit and integrity by searching for knowledge and understanding about how Indigenous HDR students can be enabled to succeed during their candidature. We also demonstrate our integrity as researchers by conducting this research honestly and by being fair and transparent about the findings of this project and by our commitment to equity, reciprocity, respect and responsibility (NHMRC, 2018). We demonstrate equity through actively engaging with Indigenous HDRs through the capacity-building workshops in which we co-teach about the pitfalls facing many Indigenous HDR students. We established equitable relationships with participants by listening to their experiences without judgement and reflecting on how we can improve Indigenous HDR students' pathways to success. We also established equitable relationships by minimising the risks of discomfort to participants during the data collection process and by ensuring the process for participants was fair. This project demonstrates reciprocity to address Universities Australia (UA) and the review of Australia's Research Training System undertaken by the Australian Council of Learned Academies' recommendation to ensure more Indigenous HDR students succeed and are represented in the academy with an academic career through the capacity-building workshops that incorporated the findings from this project for both Indigenous HDR students and their supervisors. We demonstrate respect to participants by ensuring conditions for consent were satisfied for the research and related activities including data analysis and publications. We also show respect by allowing participants to see their transcripts and modify and/or withdraw any statements (where possible). The participants' privacy was respected throughout this project. Last, we demonstrate responsible practices by providing all relevant information relating to this project and the timely dissemination of results (see Moreton-Robinson et al., 2020).

References

Behrendt, L., Larkin, S., Griew, R., & Kelly, P. (2012). *Review of higher education access and outcomes for Aboriginal and Torres Strait Islander people* (1922125253). Department of Industry, Innovation, Science, Research and Tertiary Education (Australia).

Childs, S., Finnie, R., & Martinello, F. (2016). Postsecondary student persistence and pathways: Evidence from the YITS-A in Canada. *Research in Higher Education, 58*(3), 270–294. https://doi.org/10.1007/s11162-016-9424-0

Grant, B., & McKinley, E. (2011). Colouring the pedagogy of doctoral supervision: Considering supervisor, student and knowledge through the lens of indigeneity. *Innovations in Education and Teaching International: Supervision and Cultural Difference: Rethinking Institutional Pedagogies, 48*(4), 377–386. https://doi.org/10.1080/14703297.2011.617087

Hutchings, K., Bainbridge, R., Bodle, K., & Miller, A. (2019). Determinants of attraction, retention and completion for Aboriginal and Torres Strait Islander higher degree research students: A systematic review to inform future research directions. *Research in Higher Education, 60*(2), 245–272. https://doi.org/10.1007/s11162-018-9511-5

Hutchings, K., Bodle, K. A., & Miller, A. (2018). Opportunities and resilience: Enablers to address barriers for Aboriginal and Torres Strait Islander people to commence and complete higher degree research programs. *Australian Aboriginal Studies, 2*(2), 29–49.

Laycock, A. F., Walker, D., Harrison, N., & Brands, J. (2009). *Supporting Indigenous researchers: A practical guide for supervisors*. Cooperative Research Centre for Aboriginal Health. https://www.lowitja.org.au/page/services/resources/health-services-and-workforce/workforce/Supporting-Indigenous-Researchers

Moreton-Robinson, A., Anderson, P., Blue, L., Nguyen, L., & Pham, T. (2020). *Report on Indigenous success in higher degree by research* (Prepared for Australian Government Department of Education and Training). https://eprints.qut.edu.au/199805/

National Health and Medical Research Council (NHMRC). (2018). *Ethical conduct in research with Aboriginal and Torres Strait Islander peoples and communities: Guidelines for researchers and stakeholders*. https://www.nhmrc.gov.au/about-us/resources/ethical-conduct-research-aboriginal-and-torres-strait-islander-peoples-and-communities

O'Shea, S., & Delahunty, J. (2019). What does success mean to you? Be surprised what it means to our uni students. *EduResearch Matters AARE*. https://www.aare.edu.au/blog/?p=4432

Pihama, L., Lee-Morgan, J., Smith, L. T., Tiakiwai, S. J., & Seed-Pihama, J. (2019). MAI Te Kupenga: Supporting Māori and Indigenous doctoral scholars within higher education. *AlterNative: An International Journal of Indigenous Peoples, 15*(1), 52–61.

Pinto, L. E., & Coulson, E. (2011). Social justice and the gender politics of financial literacy education. *Canadian Journal of the Association for Curriculum Studies, 9*(2), 54–85.

Raciti, M., Carter, J., Gilbey, K., & Hollinsworth, D. (2018). *The 'university place': How and why place influences the engagement and retention of Aboriginal and Torres Strait Islander university students: Final report 2017* (9781760511098). Higher Education Group, Department of Education and Training.

Schofield, T., O'Brien, R., & Gilroy, J. (2013). Indigenous higher education: Overcoming barriers to participation in research higher degree programs. *Australian Aboriginal Studies, 1*(2), 13–28.

Trudgett, M. (2011). Western places, academic spaces and Indigenous faces: Supervising Indigenous Australian postgraduate students. *Teaching in Higher Education, 16*(4), 389–399. https://doi.org/10.1080/13562517.2011.560376

Trudgett, M. (2013). Stop, collaborate and listen: A guide to seeding success for Indigenous higher degree research students. In R. Craven & J. Mooney (Eds.), *Seeding success in Indigenous Australian higher education* (Vol. 14, pp. 137–155). Emerald Group Publishing. https://doi.org/10.1108/S1479-3644(2013)0000014006

Trudgett, M. (2014). Supervision provided to Indigenous Australian doctoral students: A black and white issue. *Higher Education Research & Development, 33*(5), 1035–1048. https://doi.org/10.1080/07294360.2014.890576

Wilson, D. (2017). Supervision of Indigenous research students: Considerations for cross-cultural supervisors. *AlterNative: An International Journal of Indigenous Peoples, 13*(4), 256–265. https://doi.org/10.1177/1177180117729771

Wilson, M., Hunt, M., Richardson, L., Phillips, H., Richardson, K., & Challies, D. (2011). Āwhina: A programme for Māori and Pacific tertiary science graduate and postgraduate success. *Higher Education, 62*(6), 699–719. https://doi.org/10.1007/s10734-011-9413-3

Open Access This chapter is licensed under the terms of the Creative Commons Attribution 4.0 International License (http://creativecommons.org/licenses/by/4.0/), which permits use, sharing, adaptation, distribution and reproduction in any medium or format, as long as you give appropriate credit to the original author(s) and the source, provide a link to the Creative Commons license and indicate if changes were made.

The images or other third party material in this chapter are included in the chapter's Creative Commons license, unless indicated otherwise in a credit line to the material. If material is not included in the chapter's Creative Commons license and your intended use is not permitted by statutory regulation or exceeds the permitted use, you will need to obtain permission directly from the copyright holder.

Chapter 2
Academic Practices: Current Strategies to Attract and Retain Indigenous Higher Degree by Research Students in Australia

Abstract The number of Indigenous higher degree by research (HDR) students has increased steadily over the past decade. Support for Indigenous students from the Australian government, universities and Indigenous Support Units has been documented in Australian higher education. Unfortunately, a range of barriers continue to hinder Indigenous HDR students to completion in their research journey. Presented in this book chapter is the literature review of barriers, including lack of academic skill set and research skills to pursue a research degree program, lack of social and academic support for Indigenous HDR students, the student—supervisor relationship issues and challenges relating to health, family and community responsibilities. Simultaneously, our review identified current strategies and initiatives to retain Indigenous HDR students in their research degree programs and to support them to completion, highlighting the roles of the Indigenous Postgraduate Support Officer and the National Indigenous Research and Knowledges Network. This review, we suggest, should move further to analyse the effectiveness of current strategies and initiatives provided for Indigenous HDR students in detail to inform Indigenous students of the available support resources and how to access to these resources.

Keywords Completion · Indigenous · Higher degree by research · Participation · Retention · Strategies · Support

2.1 Introduction

Universities Australia is the peak body representing universities in Australia. They have developed an Indigenous strategy that covers 2017–2020 that aims to have retention and completion rates for Aboriginal and Torres Strait Islander (hereafter respectfully referred to as Indigenous) students equal to those of domestic non-Indigenous students in the same field of study by 2025.

The number of Indigenous Australian HDR enrolments has increased over the last decade; however, the completion rates of Indigenous HDRs have remained relatively low. Barney (2013) and Behrendt et al. (2012) concern about the under-represented participation, retention and completion rates of Indigenous HDR students in Australia. A range of factors continue to affect the retention and completion of Indigenous HDR students, including access to high-quality research supervision (Behrendt et al., 2012; Schofield et al., 2013; Trudgett, 2013, 2014). Factors including racism and discrimination and low socio-economic status affect Indigenous people's access, participation and engagement in Australian higher education (Schofield et al., 2013) and in other countries, including Canada (Childs et al., 2016), New Zealand (Schofield et al., 2013), the United States (Wilson et al., 2011) and the United Kingdom (Hutchings et al., 2019; McCulloch & Thomas, 2013). Insufficient Indigenous methodological and cultural knowledge by supervisors of Indigenous HDR students has also been found to be problematic (Grant & McKinley, 2011). As such, Indigenous HDR students have encountered plenty of challenges and barriers in their research journey (Moodie et al., 2018). However, increased and expanded support services for Indigenous students contribute to the success of Indigenous students.

This chapter provides an overview of the participation and retention of Indigenous students in Australia as well as the impediments experienced by these students, with a focus on the factors that affect their success. This chapter then considers the current academic practices to support Indigenous HDR students in research programs in Australian higher education. The review also focuses on the literature and a submitted report that analysed, evaluated and reported on how these strategies effectively increased the retention of Indigenous students, retained them in the research programs and led them to completion of their research journey.

2.2 The Participation and Retention of Indigenous Students in Australian Higher Education

A growing body in the literature has focused on explaining the failure of Indigenous HDR students (Anderson, 2016; Barney, 2016; Behrendt et al., 2012; Schofield et al., 2013) in Australian higher education. However, it is surprising to note that there are relatively few studies that have focused on understanding the factors impacting the enrolment in a research degree program, the commencement in a research candidature and the retention in an HDR program to completion of Indigenous HDR students (Hutchings et al., 2018).

The literature on the participation and retention of Indigenous students (e.g. Asmar et al., 2011; Barney, 2016, 2018; Dang et al., 2016; Moreton-Robinson et al., 2020; Oliver et al., 2013; Raciti et al., 2018) has highlighted the disparities between Indigenous and non-Indigenous students. For Australian universities to increase Indigenous students' commencement and completion rates is an existing challenge (Dang et al., 2016) despite a steady increase in the number of Indigenous students in Australia over the last decade (Moodie et al., 2018).

In a report to the Department of Education and Training (DET) about Indigenous success in higher education, Moreton-Robinson et al. (2020) reported the attendance of HDR students at Australian universities. Although the number of Indigenous students enrolled in a research degree has gradually increased since 2006, the number of students who commenced their study and completed it fluctuated in this period. The number of completions by Indigenous HDR students was very low compared to the number of enrolments and commencements during the years 2006–2017. What is interesting about this data is that the number of Indigenous HDR students enrolled in a research degree has increased in recent years (i.e. 2014–2017) with 2016 being the year with the highest completions. However, compared to the number of HDR students from the total population, the number of Indigenous HDR students is alarmingly low. The percentage of Indigenous HDR students' enrolments, commencements and completions are recorded as less than 2% of the total number of domestic students in the period 2006–2017 (see Moreton-Robinson et al., 2020). Anderson (2016, p. 223) also confirmed that "Indigenous students lag behind their non-Indigenous peers in relation to completions".

Researchers (Andersen et al., 2008; Barney, 2016; Behrendt et al., 2012; Dang et al., 2016; Hearn et al., 2019) have attempted to explore the factors causing low participation, retention and completion rates of Indigenous students in Australia. Behrendt et al. (2012) reported that the low number of Indigenous students completing Year 12 presents a primary barrier to increasing the participation of Indigenous students in higher education. Dang et al. (2016) also found that low completion rates in Year 11 and Year 12 lead to low participation and completion rates at university degree level. As a result, the participation and completion rates of Indigenous HDR students for postgraduate degrees and higher degrees by research are extremely low. In an attempt to understand why a larger proportion of Indigenous students do not choose to participate and complete a university degree that provides promising employment opportunities, Dang et al. (2016) determined a range of factors that have an impact on Indigenous students' engagement, including geographic, demographic factors, socio-political historical factors, socio-cultural factors, curricular pedagogical factors and financial and economic factors. Although Dang et al.'s study focused on Indigenous students at university level, these factors also influence the enrolments and engagement of Indigenous HDR students in Australian higher education due to the limited number of Indigenous undergraduate students.

In another study investigating factors contributing to Indigenous students' retention and attrition rates at the University of Adelaide, Hearn et al. (2019) argued that social factors and academic factors were not the factors affecting Indigenous students' decision to withdraw from their studies, but agreed with Asmar et al. (2011) that health issues, family and community responsibilities, financial difficulties, lack of support, academic disadvantage and personal well-being issues were significant factors. Asmar et al. (2011), Barney (2013), Dang et al. (2016) and Hossain et al. (2008) also added that the factor of being the first one in the family to attend university causing a burden, as well as the lack of family support for Indigenous students in engaging with their studies, could lead to Indigenous HDR students considering leaving their university. Furthermore, Indigenous students' perceptions, choices and decisions about participation in higher education were also affected by demographic factors combining with geographic factors that affect economic and cultural factors and social capital (Wilks & Wilson, 2012).

The literature on factors impacting the participation and engagement in higher education of Indigenous students has largely focused on financial issues (e.g. Asmar et al., 2011; Hossain et al., 2008; Radloff & Coates, 2010), economic and sociocultural issues (Wilks & Wilson, 2012) and issues of remoteness (Herbert et al., 2014). Several studies (Andersen et al., 2008; Behrendt et al., 2012; Hossain et al., 2008; Trudgett, 2008, 2010, 2014) also suggest having a curriculum dominated by Western practices and epistemologies, lack of institutional support, lack of university readiness, lack of a research skill set, and issues in the student–supervisor relationships have affected Indigenous university and HDR students' participation, engagement and completion rates in Australian higher education.

International higher education, including New Zealand and Pacific Island countries (Mayeda et al., 2014; McKinley et al., 2011; Theodore et al., 2017), Canada (Bailey, 2016; Childs et al., 2016) and the United States (Keith et al., 2016; Schmidtke, 2016), records the same under-represented rates of Indigenous students, and the participation rates of Indigenous HDR students are even lower. Exploring the factors impacting on the participation, retention and completion rates of HDR students, Curtis (2018, p. 122) reports that "Māori and Pacific students are the least likely to transition directly from high school to tertiary education compared to other ethnic groups" in New Zealand. As a result, this leads to low participation rates of Māori and Pacific students in postgraduate and HDR programs. In higher education in the United States, Native American (Indigenous) students have faced many challenges in pursuit of higher education. Factors such as under-preparation for academic community, social isolation, family issues and cultural differences have been identified as factors affecting Indigenous students' enrolment in higher education (Hoover & Jacobs, 1992; Hunt & Harrington, 2010, as cited in Keith et al., 2016). In Canada, Bailey (2016) reported that racism and discrimination still exist in contemporary Canadian society, which is reputedly multicultural and inclusive; however, Indigenous students are consistently faced with interpersonal discrimination, frustration with the university system and isolation issues. Furthermore, Indigenous students who experience racism and discrimination tend to drop out or withdraw from their study (Bailey, 2016).

Research has documented many factors impacting the participation, retention and completion rates of higher education for Indigenous students in Australia, New Zealand and Pacific Island countries, Canada and the United States. It is important to thoroughly understand the barriers and challenges Indigenous students have experienced that affect their success in higher education. The next section of this chapter will review the barriers and challenges Indigenous HDR students in Australia have encountered. The following section also links to the international contexts to provide an overview of impediments that restrict Indigenous HDR students' success in higher education.

2.3 Indigenous HDR Students' Barriers in Higher Education

It is now well established from a range of studies that Indigenous HDR students encounter many barriers in higher education (Barney, 2013; Moodie et al., 2018; Oliver et al., 2015; Pechenkina, 2017; Schofield et al., 2013; Trudgett, 2009; Trudgett et al., 2016). Moodie et al. (2018) synthesised the current literature and listed a range of challenges and barriers that Indigenous HDR students face in higher education, including financial hardship, culturally inappropriate support or supervision, tension between university and family–community commitments and insufficient support from university centres, units and faculties. Many recent studies have shown that financial issues (Barney, 2016; Behrendt et al., 2012; Hutchings et al., 2019; Moodie et al., 2018; Oliver et al., 2015) have been a significant factor affecting Indigenous students' well-being, and the unaffordability of staying at university has caused their decision to withdraw from their course. The literature in this book focuses on the barriers affecting Indigenous HDR students' success in completing their research study and the challenges they encountered throughout their research journey. The key barriers of Indigenous HDR students can be listed as follows: lack of an academic skill set and research skills to pursue a research degree program; lack of social and academic support for Indigenous HDR students; the student–supervisor relationship; and challenges relating to health, family and community responsibilities.

2.3.1 Lack of Academic and Research Skill Set

Lacking a research skill set, Indigenous HDR students encounter plenty of barriers in their research journey. Much of the literature discusses the types of barriers identified in the research journey of Indigenous HDR students, as well as the challenges students experience due to a lack of academic preparedness and research skills. In the review "Higher Education Access and Outcomes for Aboriginal and Torres Strait Islander People", Behrendt et al. (2012) reported that Indigenous students lack an academic skill set to pursue a university degree and a research skill set to enrol in a research degree program. Since entering university study is a major challenge, continuing to a research degree program is another level of challenge for Indigenous students (Barney, 2016).

Lacking research skills causes Indigenous HDR students to feel isolated and to be left behind from their cohorts. In the "Review of Australia's Research Training System", McGagh et al. (2016) suggest cohort support and capacity building can be improved with research training workshops, including Indigenous research methodologies to enhance Indigenous HDR students' knowledge in doing a research study. In addition, the emphasis on the academic skill-based support from supervisors was highly recommended to develop academic skills and to build confidence in doing research with Indigenous doctoral students (Moreton-Robinson et al., 2020; Trudgett, 2014).

Our research (see Chap. 1 for an overview of the research conducted) also found that many Indigenous HDR students lacked research backgrounds prior to commencing their research degrees and experienced challenges in understanding research terminology and research methods (see Chap. 5 for more details). Terms such as 'literature review', 'quantitative', 'qualitative', 'mixed methods', 'data analysis' and 'research ethics' were unfamiliar terms for some Indigenous HDR students. A lack of understanding of this basic research knowledge can confuse students and impede the collaboration with their supervisors and supervisory team.

2.3.2 Lack of Academic Support

A large and growing body of literature has investigated the support strategies for Indigenous HDR students (Anderson et al., 2021; Behrendt et al., 2012; Hutchings et al., 2018, 2019; McGagh et al., 2016; Moodie et al., 2018; Moreton-Robinson et al., 2020; Schofield et al., 2013; Trudgett, 2008, 2009, 2010, 2013). However, there has been little discussion of the role of academic support in enabling Indigenous HDR students' success in completing their research study, although Indigenous students' need for more support from academic staff has been recorded in the contemporary literature (Amundsen, 2019; Trudgett, 2009, 2010).

Trudgett (2009) addressed the issue of the lack of Indigenous academic support from Indigenous Support Units (ISUs) in Australian higher education and emphasised that "increasing the number of Indigenous academics throughout faculties and departments is critical to maintaining Indigenous representation throughout the wider university community" (p. 13). Furthermore, Trudgett also recommended that ISUs should employ more Indigenous Postgraduate Support Officers (IPSOs) to support Indigenous HDR students due to the different types of support needed by postgraduate students. Particularly, Trudgett (2009, p. 14) described how "the IPSO must possess a postgraduate qualification, ideally be an Indigenous Australian, be responsible for overseeing academic and administrative matters between students and their supervisors; organising postgraduate seminars and workshops, disseminating information about ABSTUDY, conferences and scholarships; overseeing the establishment of an Indigenous postgraduate group at the university; and organising social activities for students." Understanding the different types of support needed by Indigenous HDR students, an Indigenous Postgraduate Program Officer has been employed at the Carumba Institute, Queensland University of Technology, to provide this support as this officer's main role. The support services offered to Indigenous postgraduate students at the Carumba Institute were reported in a case study (Anderson et al., 2021) in response to the support mentioned above by Trudgett and to better support Indigenous HDR students at QUT. However, more IPSOs are required to ensure that each ISU employs at least one IPSO to specifically assist Indigenous postgraduate students enrolled within the university (Trudgett, 2009).

Academic support for Indigenous HDR students to succeed in completing a research degree also includes significant support and guidance from their supervisory team and Indigenous supervisors, particularly (Trudgett, 2009, 2013). Data from several sources have identified the dearth of Indigenous academics in Australian higher education (Harrison et al., 2017; Moreton-Robinson et al., 2020; Trudgett, 2009). Specifically, Trudgett (2009) reported that among 55 participants, only 21.8% of participants in her research had at least one Indigenous supervisor; 70.9% did not have an Indigenous supervisor. Data from the Department of Education that was discussed in Moreton-Robinson et al.'s (2020) report indicated that there were only 431 Indigenous full-time equivalent and fractional full-time Indigenous academic staff in 2018. Having an Indigenous supervisor in the supervisory team to act as a cultural advisor is critical for Indigenous HDR students. Anderson et al. (2021) revealed that it does not matter if principal supervisors are Indigenous or non-Indigenous, but HDR students should expect to have at least an Indigenous associate supervisor to provide advice and support when needed. The quality of supervision is a primary influence that contributes to the success and/or failure of Indigenous HDR students in their research journey. The student–supervisor relationship and how the quality of supervision is critical for the success of Indigenous Australian HDR students will be discussed next.

2.3.3 Issues in the Student–Supervisor Relationship

Supervision has been identified as one of the most influential factors of the likely success of Indigenous HDR students (Trudgett, 2014). More recently, attention has been focused on the quality of supervision in which the relationship between Indigenous HDR students and supervisors is critical in supporting Indigenous students to succeed in completing their research degree. A growing body of literature (McKinley et al., 2011; Trudgett, 2008, 2011, 2014; Trudgett et al., 2016) has investigated the cultural aspects affecting Indigenous HDR students and their supervisors. Surprisingly few studies have explored the issues that may arise in the Indigenous student–supervisor relationship and how these issues impact Indigenous HDR students' completion and/or academic achievements. To fill the void in this research field, this section provides an overview of student–supervisor relationship issues and reviews the influence these issues may have on Indigenous HDR students' success and/or their decision to withdraw from their research degree program.

The literature on the Indigenous student–supervisor relationship has highlighted the importance of building a good rapport based on trust and respect, to make the student–supervisor relationship work (Trudgett, 2014). From this perspective, questions have recently attracted researchers' attention about the consequences when Indigenous HDR students fail to build a good relationship with their supervisors; or if conflicts have occurred in their research cooperation; or if Indigenous HDR students cannot agree on their research project with their supervisors. However, previously, very little attention has been paid to HDR students who have issues in the relationship with their supervisory team.

Data collected in Trudgett's (2008) doctoral inquiry indicated that cultural awareness training should be mandatory for academics and should be introduced to supervisors of Indigenous students. Since cultural differences and the lack of knowledge of students' cultural background by supervisors can cause problems in the student–supervisor relationship, supervisors should have some understanding about Indigenous issues (Trudgett, 2008, 2011). Furthermore, cultural differences might affect the expectations of both supervisors and students, including research areas, research methods and students' learning approaches (Wisker et al., 2003, as cited in Trudgett, 2011). Due to the issues related to cultural difference in the relationship with supervisors, most Indigenous HDR students have indicated that they prefer to have an Indigenous supervisor in their supervisory team. As a result, including community members or elders with appropriate qualifications in the supervisory team would bring great benefits to Indigenous HDR students and limit the cultural difference issues (Trudgett, 2008, 2011, 2014).

The relationship between HDR students and their supervisors may become complicated if conflicts arise over the research intended for study. The student–supervisor relationship can develop in many different forms, including graduate supervision—the simplest research relationship, supervision plus employment of graduate students and supervision involved in an employment relationship and/or commercial research (MacDonald & Williams-Jones, 2009). In the relationship between Indigenous HDR students and supervisors, conflicts of interest may arise from their research. However, researchers have not examined this in detail. Although several studies have been conducted on the relationship between Indigenous HDR students and their supervisors (e.g. Grant & McKinley, 2011; Harrison et al., 2017; McKinley et al., 2011; Trudgett, 2014; Trudgett et al., 2016), no study has discussed the issue of different research interests, such as supervisors who drive and/or pressure students to do research in their area of expertise or for their own research interests instead of the student's. In many cases, HDR students have been allocated a supervisor instead of choosing their supervisory team, which is believed to be a cause of the conflict of research interests and the failure of cooperation between the students and their supervisors.

Detailed examination of quality supervision and the relationship between Indigenous HDR students and their supervisors by Trudgett (2011, 2014) and Trudgett et al. (2016) showed that Indigenous HDR students need a range of support systems besides quality supervision, including those discussed above, such as ISUs, IPSOs, universities and government bodies to assist Indigenous HDR students if issues arise in the relationship with their supervisory team. However, Trudgett (2013) determined that providing advice on how to handle issues pertaining to the supervisory relationship is beyond the capabilities of an IPSO. Thus, it is critical for universities in Australia to be open to involving community members who are qualified in a supervisory team to provide support for Indigenous HDR students and to listen to them when they have issues with their supervisors (Trudgett, 2014). Trudgett (2014) also suggested that providing peer networking opportunities for Indigenous doctoral students is a helpful support for Indigenous HDR students when they have problems in the relationship with their supervisors. "Ensuring all Indigenous students have information about national initiatives that will support their research capacity – most notably the National Research and Knowledges Network" (Trudgett, 2014, p. 1046) is included in the framework of best practice for the supervision of Indigenous doctoral students.

2.3.4 Issues Related to Health, Family, Community Responsibilities and Financial Hardship

Numerous studies have attempted to explain the challenges to success of Indigenous HDR students and determined that those relating to health, family and community responsibilities, finance, and issues surrounding personal well-being are barriers to the success of Indigenous HDR students (Barney, 2016; Behrendt et al., 2012; Hearn et al., 2019; Trudgett, 2014). Trudgett (2014) listed a range of barriers to success of Indigenous doctoral students, including family responsibilities, divorce, a partner or family who fails to understand the PhD journey, community responsibilities, financial needs and loneliness of the journey. Cardilini et al. (2021) also found that the issues in the relationship with supervisors also caused mental health issues for Indigenous HDR students.

Regarding family responsibilities, Behrendt et al. (2012) reported this can be problematic because of a lack of advice from family members and an absence of Indigenous role models for Indigenous students as they are the first ones attend university in the family. In the same vein, Rochecouste et al. (2017) and Hutchings et al. (2018) also indicated that many Indigenous students who are first in the family to attend university have certain obligations in relation to family, and this and the lack of family support can affect their success at university. Furthermore, "the obligations Indigenous students have to care for extended family extended members which provides an additional burden in terms of finances and time can contribute to non-completion" (Rochecouste et al., 2017, p. 2086). In line with Rochecouste et al.'s study, Hearn et al. (2019) determined that there is an association between caring for their parents, children and extended family and the likelihood of withdrawing from study of Indigenous HDR students. This can be particularly difficult for mature age Indigenous students who were recorded as often overwhelmed with day-to-day matters on the family and community front, which may lead to their withdrawal from their research study (Devlin, 2009; as cited in Hearn et al., 2019).

The literature on barriers to success of Indigenous students has highlighted health issues as an impediment (Hearn et al., 2019; Paradies, 2006; Pechenkina & Anderson, 2011; Pechenkina et al., 2011; Trudgett et al., 2016; Wilks & Wilson, 2015). Particularly, ill health is one of the principal reasons for deferring and non-completion of Indigenous students (Asmar et al., 2011). Ill health is identified to be an additional burden along with other impediments such as financial hardship, family and community responsibilities and the lack of social support that restricts Indigenous students' access to university (Trudgett et al., 2016). Although Trudgett et al. (2016) believe that "the effects of ill health are not necessarily immediately remedied by educational progress" (p. 75), Barney (2016) states that due to a myriad of challenges Indigenous students face in the undergraduate level, to do HDR is another level of challenge.

A considerable body of literature has demonstrated that financial hardship remains a significant issue for Indigenous students' success in completing their studies (Barney, 2016; Behrendt et al., 2012; Hearn et al., 2019; Hutchings et al., 2018; McGagh et al., 2016; Pechenkina & Anderson, 2011; Trudgett, 2014). In all the various factors that have been found to be barriers restricting Indigenous students' access to Australian higher education system and hindering their success in completing university courses, a postgraduate program and/or a doctoral degree, "financial hardship remains on the top of the list as the main barrier to Indigenous educational achievement" (Pechenkina & Anderson, 2011, p. 11). In accordance with Trudgett (2014) and Hearn et al. (2019), Barney (2016) determined that financial hardship is the reason why the number of Indigenous students transitioning from undergraduate degrees to HDR is so low; and financial hardship is the main reason why HDR students quit their studies. Barney also indicated that although there is financial support for Indigenous students, the scholarships are too low in financial value and are not available for part-time students. In addition, Indigenous students who enrol in a HDR program are usually mature age and these students usually have more financial and family responsibilities (James et al., 2008). Collectively, these studies determined that financial problems are the main barrier that can limit Indigenous students' access to higher education and can lead to withdrawing because of financial hardship and influencing Indigenous students' educational pathway (Dang et al., 2016).

Considering all of this evidence, it seems that Indigenous HDR students may encounter a wide range of barriers that can hinder their success in completing a master's or doctoral degree in Australia. Barriers, such as lack of an academic skill set and the research skills to pursue a research degree program, the lack of social and academic support for Indigenous HDR students, issues in the student–supervisor relationship and challenges relating to health, family and community responsibilities and financial hardship are all significant challenges for Indigenous HDR students' success. This chapter will also review the current strategies used in Australian higher education to support Indigenous students' success in a HDR program.

2.4 Current Academic Practices to Support Indigenous HDR Students

The academic literature across this field of research has recorded a range of strategies for supporting Indigenous HDR students to increase their participation in Australian higher education. The number of Indigenous HDR students has also increased steadily in recent years. However, Indigenous HDR students, as mentioned above,

2.4 Current Academic Practices to Support Indigenous HDR Students

continue to encounter barriers to completion, highlighting in particular the impact of the absence of a research background, inadequate support, potential issues in the relationship with supervisory team and the issues related to health, family and community responsibilities and financial support. In terms of these barriers, this section will review the current strategies that are used to support Indigenous HDR students to succeed in completing their research degree. The review is also seeking evidence in the current literature that reveals whether the current support strategies are effective in attracting more Indigenous HDR students to enrol in a research degree in Australia, such as masters by research or a doctoral degree.

In response to the issues of the absence of a research background and lack of support for Indigenous HDR students in higher education, a range of initiatives have been implemented to improve their research capacity (Behrendt et al., 2012; Hutchings et al., 2018, 2019; McGagh et al., 2016; Moodie et al., 2018; Trudgett, 2009, 2010). In particular, the National Indigenous Research and Knowledges Network (NIRAKN), funded by the ARC, was established in 2012 under the Special Research Initiative for Aboriginal and Torres Strait Islander Researchers' network. The NIRAKN provided Indigenous HDR students with support 'to develop a critical mass of skilled, informed and qualified Aboriginal and Torres Strait Islander researchers who can address the urgent needs of our communities through the delivery of culturally appropriate research' (Anderson, 2020, p.2). However, McGagh et al. (2016) indicated that the NIRAKN program alone is still insufficient to assist Indigenous HDR students and/or researchers across the country to overcome the deficiency in research capacity. McGagh et al. also suggested that taking up Behrendt et al.'s (2012) recommendations would be a practical approach to address this issue. Further, the funding of a targeted research training program for Indigenous HDR programs and activities was an effective strategy to improve research capacity for Indigenous HDR students (University of Newcastle, 2015).

To support Indigenous HDR students holistically, the support provided by government, universities and ISUs is critical as they are the three main bodies responsible for supporting Indigenous postgraduate students in Australia (Trudgett, 2009). In addition, Trudgett (2014) also determined that supervisors and good supervision play a key role in supporting Indigenous HDR students to completion. This view is supported by Moreton-Robinson et al. (2020), who reported that good practice in supervision highlighted the factors of disciplinary expertise, good understanding of the HDR process, respect for students' knowledge and cultures, supervisors' availability and interest in students' research, as well as supervisors' willingness to develop a good rapport and a reciprocal relationship with HDR students. Furthermore, improving cohort support is a productive approach in assisting Indigenous students' networking to share experiences in their research journey and help deal with isolation (McGagh et al., 2016).

Trudgett (2009) mentioned the importance of ISUs at Australian universities and recommended that all ISUs should have an IPSO. The ISUs have been recorded by the National Indigenous Australians Agency. However, IPSOs have seldom been documented until Anderson et al. (2021) reported a case study at the Carumba Institute, Queensland University of Technology, about support services offered to Indigenous postgraduate students. An IPSO whose main role is to offer support to Indigenous postgraduate students is employed at the Carumba Institute.

Unfortunately, to resolve issues that may arise in the relationship between Indigenous HDR students and their supervisors is not always appropriate for an IPSO (Trudgett, 2013). Recommendations such as including qualified Indigenous people from the Community in the supervisory team (Trudgett, 2014), having at least one Indigenous associate supervisor and having support from Indigenous centres and convenors (Anderson et al., 2021) have been proposed. Research to date has not yet determined the effectiveness of ISUs in assisting Indigenous HDR students to resolve the problems in the student–supervisor relationship. Nor is there any suggestion of a negative influence on their study once Indigenous students report problems to an ISU or faculty. However, whether the problems in the relationship with Indigenous HDR students' supervisor are resolved or not, these can still affect the psychological well-being of Indigenous HDR students and all HDR students in general, possibly causing uncomfortable feelings and a lack of confidence in working with their supervisors.

Various support strategies have been employed over the past decade to assist Indigenous HDR students to succeed in their research journey. Although the effectiveness of these strategies, such as including an Indigenous supervisor in the supervisory team, establishing an ISU, having an IPSO and providing scholarships and bursaries to Indigenous HDR students, has not been fully evaluated, it has been documented that the number of Indigenous HDR students' enrolments and completion has been steadily increased during 2008–2018 (Department of Education, 2019; Universities Australia, 2020). The "Indigenous Strategy Annual Report, January 2020 by Universities Australia and the Indigenous Higher Degrees by Research", a report by the Department of Education (2019), contains more details and statistical information about the participation, retention and success of Indigenous students in Australian higher education.

2.5 Summary

Supporting Indigenous students effectively is key to enabling them to succeed in completing a higher education research degree and to close the employment gap between Indigenous and non-Indigenous students. The growth rates in the participation, completion and retention of Indigenous HDR students in recent years have demonstrated that support strategies from the government, universities and ISUs have been productive. Furthermore, a thorough understanding of and preparation for HDR study will increase the number of Indigenous students' completion. We found that the capacity-building workshops provided by NIRAKN have played a crucial role in preparing and developing Indigenous HDR students' research skills over the past few years. In the next chapter, we present the findings and insights from the NIRAKN capacity-building workshops and the benefits these provided to the Indigenous HDR students who participated.

References

Amundsen, D. (2019). Student voice and agency for Indigenous Māori students in higher education transitions. *Australian Journal of Adult Learning, 59*(3), 405.

Andersen, C., Bunda, T., & Walter, M. (2008). Indigenous higher education: The role of universities in releasing the potential. *The Australian Journal of Indigenous Education, 37*(1), 1–8.

Anderson, I. (2016). Indigenous Australians and higher education: The contemporary policy agenda. In A. Harvey, C. Burnheim, & M. Brett (Eds.), *Student equity in Australian higher education: Twenty-five years of a fair chance for all* (pp. 221–239). Springer Singapore. https://doi.org/10.1007/978-981-10-0315-8_13

Anderson, P. (2020). *NIRAKN annual report for 2020*. https://www.nirakn.edu.au/

Anderson, P., Pham, T., Blue, L., & Fox, A. (2021). Supporting Indigenous higher degree by research students in higher education. In H. Huijser, M. Kek, & F. F. Padró (Eds.), *Student support services* (pp. 1–14). Springer Singapore. https://doi.org/10.1007/978-981-13-3364-4_39-1

Asmar, C., Page, S., & Radloff, A. (2011). Dispelling myths: Indigenous students' engagement with university. *AUSSE Research Briefings, 10*, 1–15.

Bailey, K. A. (2016). Racism within the Canadian university: Indigenous students' experiences. *Ethnic and Racial Studies, 39*(7), 1261–1279. https://doi.org/10.1080/01419870.2015.1081961

Barney, K. (2013). 'Taking your mob with you': Giving voice to the experiences of Indigenous Australian postgraduate students. *Higher Education Research & Development, 32*(4), 515–528. https://doi.org/10.1080/07294360.2012.696186

Barney, K. (2016). *Pathways to postgraduate study for Indigenous Australian students: Enhancing the transition to higher degrees by research*. Australian Government. https://altf.org/wp-content/uploads/2016/08/Barney_NTF_Report_2016.pdf

Barney, K. (2018). Community gets you through: Success factors contributing to the retention of Aboriginal and Torres Strait Islander higher degree by research (HDR) students. *Student Success, 9*(4), 13–23. https://doi.org/10.5204/ssj.v9i4.654

Behrendt, L., Larkin, S., Griew, R., & Kelly, P. (2012). *Review of higher education access and outcomes for Aboriginal and Torres Strait Islander people* (1922125253). Department of Industry, Innovation, Science, Research and Tertiary Education (Australia).

Cardilini, A. P. A., Risely, A., & Richardson, M. F. (2021). Supervising the PhD: Identifying common mismatches in expectations between candidate and supervisor to improve research training outcomes. *Higher Education Research & Development*, 1–15. https://doi.org/10.1080/07294360.2021.1874887

Childs, S., Finnie, R., & Martinello, F. (2016). Postsecondary student persistence and pathways: Evidence from the YITS-A in Canada. *Research in Higher Education, 58*(3), 270–294. https://doi.org/10.1007/s11162-016-9424-0

Curtis, E. T. (2018). Vision 20:20 and Indigenous health workforce development: Institutional strategies and initiatives to attract underrepresented students into elite courses. In M. Shah & J. McKay (Eds.), *Achieving equity and quality in higher education: Global perspectives in an era of widening participation* (pp. 119–142). Springer. https://doi.org/10.1007/978-3-319-78316-1_6

Dang, T. K. A., Vitartas, P., Ambrose, K., & Millar, H. (2016). Improving the participation and engagement of Aboriginal and Torres Strait Islander students in business education. *Journal of Higher Education Policy and Management, 38*(1), 19–38. https://doi.org/10.1080/1360080X.2015.1126891

Department of Education. (2019). *Indigenous students in higher degrees by research. Statistical report, August 2019*. Australian Government. https://www.dese.gov.au/download/4830/indigenous-students-higher-degrees-research/7202/document/pdf

Devlin, M. (2009). Indigenous higher education student equity: Focusing on what works. *Australian Journal of Indigenous Education, 38*(1), 1–8. https://doi.org/10.1375/S1326011100000533

Grant, B., & McKinley, E. (2011). Colouring the pedagogy of doctoral supervision: Considering supervisor, student and knowledge through the lens of indigeneity. *Innovations in Education and Teaching International, 48*(4), 377–386. https://doi.org/10.1080/14703297.2011.617087

Harrison, N., Trudgett, M., & Page, S. (2017). The dissertation examination: Identifying critical factors in the success of Indigenous Australian doctoral students. *Assessment & Evaluation in Higher Education, 42*(1), 115–127. https://doi.org/10.1080/02602938.2015.1085488

Hearn, S., Benton, M., Funnell, S., & Marmolejo-Ramos, F. (2019). Investigation of the factors contributing to Indigenous students' retention and attrition rates at the University of Adelaide. *The Australian Journal of Indigenous Education,* 1–9.

Herbert, J., McInerney, D. M., Fasoli, L., Stephenson, P., & Ford, L. (2014). Indigenous secondary education in the Northern Territory: Building for the future. *The Australian Journal of Indigenous Education, 43*(2), 85–95. https://doi.org/10.1017/jie.2014.17

Hoover, J. J., & Jacobs, C. C. (1992). A survey of American Indian college students: Perceptions toward their study skills/college life. *Journal of American Indian Education,* 21–29.

Hossain, D., Gorman, D., Williams-Mozely, J., & Garvey, D. (2008). Bridging the gap: Identifying needs and aspirations of Indigenous students to facilitate their entry into university. *The Australian Journal of Indigenous Education, 37*(1), 9–17. https://doi.org/10.1017/S1326011100016045

Hunt, B., & Harrington, C. F. (2010). The impending educational crisis for American Indians: Higher education at the crossroads. *Indigenous Policy Journal, 21*(3), 1–13.

Hutchings, K., Bainbridge, R., Bodle, K., & Miller, A. (2019). Determinants of attraction, retention and completion for Aboriginal and Torres Strait Islander higher degree research students: A systematic review to inform future research directions. *Research in Higher Education, 60*(2), 245–272. https://doi.org/10.1007/s11162-018-9511-5

Hutchings, K., Bodle, K. A., & Miller, A. (2018). Opportunities and resilience: Enablers to address barriers for Aboriginal and Torres Strait Islander people to commence and complete higher degree research programs. *Australian Aboriginal Studies, 2.*

James, R., Bexley, E., Anderson, A., Devlin, M., Garnett, R., Marginson, S., & Maxwell, L. (2008). *Participation and equity: A review of the participation in higher education of people from low socioeconomic backgrounds and Indigenous people. Report prepared for Universities Australia: Centre for the Study of Higher Education, University of Melbourne.* Centre for the Study of Higher Education. https://dro.deakin.edu.au/view/DU:30006777?print_friendly=true

Keith, J. F., Stastny, S. N., & Brunt, A. (2016). Barriers and strategies for success for American Indian college students: A review. *Journal of College Student Development, 57*(6), 698–714. https://doi.org/10.1353/csd.2016.0069

MacDonald, C., & Williams-Jones, B. (2009). Supervisor–student relations: Examining the spectrum of conflicts of interest in bioscience laboratories. *Accountability in Research, 16*(2), 106–126. https://doi.org/10.1080/08989620902855033

Mayeda, D. T., Keil, M., Dutton, H. D., & Ofamo'Oni, I.-F.-H. (2014). 'You've gotta set a precedent': Māori and Pacific voices on student success in higher education. *AlterNative: An International Journal of Indigenous Peoples, 10*(2), 165–179. https://doi.org/10.1177/117718011401000206

McCulloch, A., & Thomas, L. (2013). Widening participation to doctoral education and research degrees: A research agenda for an emerging policy issue. *Higher Education Research & Development, 32*(2), 214–227. https://doi.org/10.1080/07294360.2012.662630

McGagh, J., Marsh, H., Western, M., Thomas, P., Hastings, A., Mihailova, M., & Wenham, M. (2016). *Review of Australia's research training system.* https://acola.org/wp-content/uploads/2018/08/saf13-review-research-training-system-report.pdf

McKinley, E., Grant, B., Middleton, S., Irwin, K., & Williams, L. R. T. (2011). Working at the interface: Indigenous students' experience of undertaking doctoral studies in Aotearoa New Zealand. *Equity & Excellence in Education: Examining Doctoral Education Across Academic Disciplines Using a Social Justice Perspective, 44*(1), 115–132. https://doi.org/10.1080/10665684.2010.540972

Moodie, N., Ewen, S., McLeod, J., & Platania-Phung, C. (2018). Indigenous graduate research students in Australia: A critical review of the research. *Higher Education Research & Development, 37*(4), 805–820. https://doi.org/10.1080/07294360.2018.1440536

References

Moreton-Robinson, A., Anderson, P., Blue, L., Nguyen, L., & Pham, T. (2020). *Report on Indigenous success in higher degree by research: Prepared for Australian Government Department of Education and Training*. https://eprints.qut.edu.au/199805/

Oliver, R., Grote, E., Rochecouste, J., & Dann, T. (2015). Indigenous student perspectives on support and impediments at university. *The Australian Journal of Indigenous Education, 45*(1), 23–35. https://doi.org/10.1017/jie.2015.16

Oliver, R., Rochecouste, J., & Grote, E. (2013). *The transition of Aboriginal and Torres Strait Islander students into higher education*. Office for Learning and Teaching, NSW Department of Education.

Paradies, Y. C. (2006). Beyond black and white: Essentialism, hybridity and indigeneity. *Journal of Sociology, 42*(4), 355–367. https://doi.org/10.1177/1440783306069993

Pechenkina, E. (2017). 'It becomes almost an act of defiance': Indigenous Australian transformational resistance as a driver of academic achievement. *Race, Ethnicity and Education, 20*(4), 463–477. https://doi.org/10.1080/13613324.2015.1121220

Pechenkina, E., & Anderson, I. (2011). *Background paper on Indigenous Australian higher education: Trends, initiatives and policy implications* (Prepared for the Review of Higher Education Access and Outcomes for Aboriginal and Torres Strait Islander). Department of Education, Employment and Workplace Relations.

Pechenkina, E., Kowal, E., & Paradies, Y. (2011). Indigenous Australian students' participation rates in higher education: Exploring the role of universities. *The Australian Journal of Indigenous Education, 40*, 59–68. https://doi.org/10.1375/ajie.40.59

Raciti, M., Carter, J., Gilbey, K., & Hollinsworth, D. (2018). *The 'university place': How and why place influences the engagement and retention of Aboriginal and Torres Strait Islander university students: Final report 2017* (9781760511098). Australian Government.

Radloff, A., & Coates, H. (2010). *Doing more for learning: Enhancing engagement and outcomes: Australasian survey of student engagement: Australasian student engagement report*. Australian Council of Educational Research.

Rochecouste, J., Oliver, R., Bennell, D., Anderson, R., Cooper, I., & Forrest, S. (2017). Teaching Australian Aboriginal higher education students: What should universities do? *Studies in Higher Education, 42*(11), 2080–2098. https://doi.org/10.1080/03075079.2015.1134474

Schmidtke, C. (2016). The role of academic student services in the retention of American Indian students at a sub-baccalaureate technical college. *Journal of Career and Technical Education, 31*(1), 33–60.

Schofield, T., O'Brien, R., & Gilroy, J. (2013). Indigenous higher education: Overcoming barriers to participation in research higher degree programs. *Australian Aboriginal Studies, 2*, 13–28.

Theodore, R., Gollop, M., Tustin, K., Taylor, N., Kiro, C., Taumoepeau, M., Kakaua, J., Hunter, J., & Poulton, R. (2017). Māori university success: What helps and hinders qualification completion. *AlterNative: An International Journal of Indigenous Peoples, 13*(2), 122–130. https://doi.org/10.1177/1177180117700799

Trudgett, M. (2008). *An investigation into the support provided to Indigenous postgraduate students in Australia* [Doctoral thesis]. https://hdl.handle.net/1959.11/4061

Trudgett, M. (2009). Build it and they will come: Building the capacity of Indigenous units in universities to provide better support for Indigenous Australian postgraduate students. *Australian Journal of Indigenous Education, 38*, 9–18.

Trudgett, M. (2010). Supporting the learning needs of Indigenous Australians in higher education: How can they be best achieved? *International Journal of Learning, 17*(3), 351–361.

Trudgett, M. (2011). Western places, academic spaces and Indigenous faces: Supervising Indigenous Australian postgraduate students. *Teaching in Higher Education, 16*(4), 389–399. https://doi.org/10.1080/13562517.2011.560376

Trudgett, M. (2013). Stop, collaborate and listen: A guide to seeding success for Indigenous higher degree research students. In R. Craven & J. Mooney (Eds.), *Seeding success in Indigenous Australian higher education* (Vol. 14, pp. 137–155). Emerald Group Publishing. https://doi.org/10.1108/S1479-3644(2013)0000014006

Trudgett, M. (2014). Supervision provided to Indigenous Australian doctoral students: A black and white issue. *Higher Education Research & Development, 33*(5), 1035–1048. https://doi.org/10.1080/07294360.2014.890576

Trudgett, M., Page, S., & Harrison, N. (2016). Brilliant minds: A snapshot of successful Indigenous Australian doctoral students. *The Australian Journal of Indigenous Education, 45*(1), 70–79. https://doi.org/10.1017/jie.2016.8

Universities Australia. (2020). *Indigenous strategy annual report*. https://www.universitiesaustralia.edu.au/wp-content/uploads/2020/02/Indigenous-strategy-second-annual-report.pdf

University of Newcastle. (2015). *Written submission to the review of Australia's research training system*. Australian Council of Learned Academies.

Wilks, J., & Wilson, K. (2012). Going on to uni? Access and participation in university for students from backgrounds of disadvantage. *Journal of Higher Education Policy and Management, 34*(1), 79–90. https://doi.org/10.1080/1360080X.2012.642335

Wilks, J., & Wilson, K. (2015). A profile of the Aboriginal and Torres Strait Islander higher education student population. *Australian Universities' Review, 57*(2), 17–30.

Wilson, M., Hunt, M., Richardson, L., Phillips, H., Richardson, K., & Challies, D. (2011). Āwhina: A programme for Māori and Pacific tertiary science graduate and postgraduate success. *Higher Education, 62*(6), 699–719. https://doi.org/10.1007/s10734-011-9413-3

Wisker, G., Waller, S., Richter, U., Robinson, G., Trafford, V., Wicks, K., & Warnes, M. (2003, July). *On nurturing hedgehogs: Developments online for distance and offshore supervision* [Paper presentation]. Learning for an Unknown Future: 26th HERDSA Annual Conference, Christchurch, New Zealand.

Open Access This chapter is licensed under the terms of the Creative Commons Attribution 4.0 International License (http://creativecommons.org/licenses/by/4.0/), which permits use, sharing, adaptation, distribution and reproduction in any medium or format, as long as you give appropriate credit to the original author(s) and the source, provide a link to the Creative Commons license and indicate if changes were made.

The images or other third party material in this chapter are included in the chapter's Creative Commons license, unless indicated otherwise in a credit line to the material. If material is not included in the chapter's Creative Commons license and your intended use is not permitted by statutory regulation or exceeds the permitted use, you will need to obtain permission directly from the copyright holder.

Chapter 3
Capacity-Building Support for Indigenous HDR Students via the National Indigenous Research and Knowledges Network

Abstract Since 2013, Indigenous higher degree by research (HDR) students have had an opportunity to participate in capacity-building workshops conducted by the National Indigenous Research and Knowledges Network (NIRAKN). The workshops included basic information about completing a research degree, including how to navigate academia, how to read and write critically and an introduction to Indigenous research methodologies. In this chapter, an overview of what NIRAKN set out to achieve and what has been accomplished is discussed. Evaluation forms completed by Indigenous HDR students ($n = 78$) who attended capacity-building workshops were analysed to understand what students found to be beneficial when participating in NIRAKN events. Here, we share the findings and offer insights into ways higher education institutions can support Indigenous HDR students in the successful completion of their degrees.

Keywords Capacity building · Indigenous HDR students · Higher degree by research · University · Research

3.1 Introduction

> Thank you for giving Indigenous PhD students like myself, the wonderful opportunities NIRAKN offer (OLS1_IndigenousHDR10).

From 2013 to 2021, Indigenous HDR students have had the opportunity to be a part of the National Indigenous Research and Knowledges Network (NIRAKN). NIRAKN is in its legacy phase with funding having been extended until the end of 2022 to complete associated research projects and to develop an online Website where the capacity-building resources will be stored and made freely available to anyone.

NIRAKN was made possible by funding awarded from the Australian Research Council's Special Research Initiative (SRI120100005) that was applied for by Distinguished Professor Moreton-Robinson. Moreton-Robinson was Director of NIRAKN from 2013 to late 2017 when Professor Peter Anderson became Director of NIRAKN. Professor Anderson, who is based at the Queensland University of Technology, is the National Hub Leader who has responsibilities for Queensland, Victoria, Tasmania, Canberra and Western Australia. Associate Professor Linda Ford is State Hub Leader for South Australia and the Northern Territory. Pro-Vice Chancellor (Indigenous Strategy) Dr. Leanne Holt is State Hub Leader for New South Wales. All of the Hub Leaders also had Chief Investigators in NIRAKN who worked with them to deliver the capacity-building workshops and/or conduct research.

NIRAKN's stated aims are as follows:

1. Establish a coterie of skilled, qualified Indigenous researchers by creating pathways from undergraduate to postgraduate studies to establish a regenerative pipeline of new researchers, across institutions, the nation and fields of critical research importance.
2. Deliver a program of research capacity building in order to develop a critical mass of multidisciplinary, qualified Indigenous researchers to meet the compelling research needs of our communities.
3. Connect Indigenous researchers nationally and internationally to develop culturally supportive, inclusive research environments, which enable cross fertilisation of ideas and provide platforms for new Indigenous multidisciplinary research.
4. Begin setting the Indigenous research agenda by applying Indigenous knowledges and expertise to multidisciplinary, collaborative projects directed at compelling the research needed to inform community and government policy and program delivery.
5. Develop an ongoing, integrated research program of collaborations with partner organisations through the ARC, NHMRC, government, industry, community and philanthropic grant funding.
6. Achieve national and international recognition as the centre of Australian Indigenous research expertise, knowledge and innovation (Moreton-Robinson, 2016, p. 3).

In this chapter, we describe the capacity-building workshops that were an essential component of NIRAKN (Aim 2 above). Since 2013, these workshops have been offered face to face to Aboriginal and/or Torres Strait Islander (hereafter Indigenous) HDR students across Australia. State Hub Leaders were responsible for offering the capacity-building workshops to Indigenous HDR students within the state(s) and/or territory. Funding was provided by the National Hub based at Queensland University of Technology (QUT) to State Hub Leaders for two purposes: first, State Hub Leaders received funding to complete an agreed-upon research project; and second, funding was provided to run capacity-building workshops (Anderson, 2020). Funding to deliver capacity-building workshops included providing meals during the training and all travel and accommodation costs for participants.

Professor Peter Anderson commenced the role of NIRAKN Director in late 2017 and Dr. Levon Blue commenced as the NIRAKN Coordinator in January 2018. All data collected and analysed in this book is from 2018 to 2021 only as that was when ethical approval was sought and gained for various research projects relating to the needs and experiences of Indigenous HDR students.

In 2018, all State Hub Leaders attended a train-the-trainer workshop where they were provided with a hard drive that included all of the capacity-building resources and evaluation forms. The last offering of face-to-face capacity-building workshops occurred in 2020 by the state and/or territory Hub Leaders who still had capacity-building funds. The travel restrictions in place due to the COVID-19 pandemic meant that some workshops occurred online. In 2020, a decision to move the capacity-building workshops to online offerings was made with approval by the ARC representatives. The revised NIRAKN Website that include the capacity-building workshops is available at www.nirakn.edu.au. To contextualise the NIRAKN workshops, an overview of what they entailed is discussed. However, before focusing on the workshop, we will identify the methods and data analysis used.

3.2 Methodology and Data Analysis

Indigenous research methodologies that focus on relationship building, reciprocity, relational accountability and respect (Wilson, 2008) have guided our research practices. The research was made possible through funding provided by the ARC and also through the relationships that were formed with Indigenous HDR students attending NIRAKN capacity-building workshops. The research projects conducted have provided opportunities to develop trust, relational accountabilities and a sense of equal research partnerships as both the researchers and the participants (Indigenous HDR students) contribute towards the goal of understanding how more Indigenous HDR students can experience success in their study goals.

Informing this chapter are evaluations completed during the QLD/NSW 2018 capacity-building workshops at QUT and the capacity-building workshop on the Gold Coast ($n = 65$) and the NIRAKN evaluation form completed in 2021 ($n = 13$) (see Moreton-Robinson et al., 2020). The pen-and-paper evaluation forms were completed by Indigenous HDR students at the end of the capacity-building workshops. The forms were then scanned into NVivo and coded to identify themes. The online NIRAKN evaluation survey was developed using the Qualtrics online platform. The responses from the capacity-building workshops were uploaded in NVivo so that they could be read, tagged and coded into themes. The online survey evaluations were smaller in number and were analysed using Excel, where the responses were read, and text was highlighted and placed into themes. In the next section, we report on the themes from all sources of data (see Table 3.1).

3.3 The Workshops

> Just that I wish there were more NIRAKN workshops offered each year! They really are invaluable (WEF_IndigenousHDR3).

Prior to the NIRAKN capacity-building workshops, few such opportunities were available for Indigenous HDR students (Behrendt et al., 2012). Thus, Moreton-Robinson (2016) advocated that "University investment in stable and properly funded

Table 3.1 Datasets relating to NIRAKN

Dataset number	Type (written evaluation form, group and/or online survey)	Year collected	What it is and who it includes	Number of participants	Referred to in text as
1	Written evaluation form (qualitative)	2018	NIRAKN workshop evaluations (Indigenous HDR students)	65	WEF_IndigenousHDR#
2	Online survey (qualitative with quantitative demographic information)	2021	NIRAKN evaluation (former Indigenous HDR students)	13	OLS1_IndigenousHDR#
Total				78	

Indigenous research and research capacity building is critical to achieving Indigenous research success" (p. 9). Since 2013, Indigenous HDR students have had access to the capacity-building workshops that focused on their needs and experiences and provided opportunities for them and Indigenous academics to network at NIRAKN events and conferences. Since NIRAKN is a national initiative, State Hub Leaders were established to focus on particular states to provide capacity-building training workshops.

Each State Hub Leader conducted their capacity-building workshops according to the needs of the HDR students enrolled at the universities they engaged with. In this chapter, we are referring to the NIRAKN capacity-building workshops that were run by the National NIRAKN Hub at the Queensland University of Technology (QUT) for which Professor Peter Anderson was the State Hub Leader.

At the national hub, three workshops were offered. The first was an introductory three-day workshop for students in the early stages of their candidature. Presenters covered topics such as graduate capabilities, dissertation examination, developing research questions, conducting database searches, conference presentation protocols, using EndNote, project management, applying for grants, practical writing tips, value of publishing and career choice pathways. A two-day masterclass on Indigenous research methodologies was also offered. This masterclass included topics such as 'Introduction to Indigenous Research Methodologies', 'Why Indigenous Research Methodologies', 'Rigor in Research Using Indigenous Research Methodologies', 'Indigenous Standpoint Theory', 'Indigenous Women's Standpoint Theory', 'Indigenous Research Methodologies: Culture and Methods', 'Focus on Indigenous Researchers' and examples of using Indigenous Research Methodologies and Methods while designing and managing successful research projects. A one-day critical reading workshop was also offered and covered topics such as how to read critically, including a practical example and opportunities to read your own article and identify problems, as well as tips for reading, thinking and writing critically. Although topics covered by the capacity-building workshops (with the exception of the Indigenous Research Methodologies masterclass) are offered at most higher education institutions, it was noted that Indigenous HDR students often did not attend these seminars. Therefore, there continues to be an ongoing demand by Indigenous HDR students to attend the capacity-building workshops offered by NIRAKN, in addition to those already available at the university. Another important reason Indigenous HDR students attended the NIRAKN workshops was because it provided them with an opportunity to network with other Indigenous HDR students from other universities and/or Indigenous academics from around Australia.

3.4 Networking

An additional outcome of attending the NIRAKN capacity-building workshops was the opportunity to form support networks over the years. These Indigenous postgraduate networks "enabled peer support and fostered an exchange of ideas" (Moreton-Robinson, 2016, p. 4). There have also been opportunities for Indigenous HDR students and Indigenous academics to come together at conferences (see Anderson, 2019, 2020). Providing these networking events has enabled Indigenous HDR students to see a possible future for themselves in academia. During these events and in the capacity-building workshops, time was spent answering students' questions about academia, including how to navigate higher education without having academic capital. By *academic capital*, we are referring to a student's ability to navigate academia with an understanding of how the system works and with the belief that they belong.

A student who attended the capacity-building workshops at QUT stated that "NIRAKN is where we all, as Indigenous researchers should start!" (WEF_IndigenousHDR1). They questioned why they were not informed about NIRAKN earlier and stated that "the insider knowledge that was shared, was very, very much appreciated. It has made me feel my journey is going along well and I am on track" (WEF_IndigenousHDR1). The insider knowledge the participant referred to includes the informal conversations the facilitators had with HDR students about what takes place in higher education, including how theses are examined, how researchers are ranked in internal research databases, and how Indigenous people are targeted as Chief Investigators (CIs) for ARC grants and/or to co-author publications that involve Indigenous matters. The academic capital shared and acquired at NIRAKN workshops was another outcome of the workshops.

3.5 Do I Belong?

Since many participants mentioned they did not have conversations with friends and family about their HDR journey, NIRAKN was valued for "being able to do it with qualified Indigenous peoples" (OLS1_IndigenousHDR13). Some participants mentioned that at times they felt like they did not belong in higher education. To address this, we discussed imposter syndrome and shared how many academics still have imposter syndrome long after receiving their doctoral degree. 'Imposter syndrome' was first coined by Clance and Imes (1978) and is about the feelings an individual (in their study, it was about women) has about not really belonging as an academic despite having the academic qualifications and believing that they have been able to fool individuals that they belong in academia. In a more recent paper, Edwards (2019) stated that "self-doubt was illustrative of systematic issues within the broader social context; and imposter syndrome, stereotype threat, and intersectionality are three lenses that offer language to examine the theoretical constructs that were at play" (p. 23). With many Indigenous HDR, students come into academia with intersections of marginalised identities, including a low-income background and being first-generation students and Indigenous, the unfamiliar territory can come with feelings associated with not belonging and needing to tread softly so that no one discovers that you 'fooled' your supervisors into taking you on as a HDR student.

After having open conversations with HDR students about imposter syndrome, one participant stated that "being aware of imposter syndrome is important and when these feelings/fears come over me – and then what steps I need to take to address it". Discussing the concept of imposter syndrome and normalising the feeling reassured participants that they belonged in academia.

3.6 Realising I Do Belong

> It's such a great program and is so deadly being able to meet up with other First Nations students so you don't feel so alone (WEF_IndigenousHDR13).

Edwards (2019) reflected on what was believed a scholar looked like (which was far from what was envisioned—for example, a laboratory coat, Albert Einstein) and realised that it was important for students to reconceptualise the definition of a scholar in order to come to the realisation that they are indeed a scholar. Realising that you do belong in academia is required to enact agency in academic settings. Agency is discussed in the next chapter, and it has to do with feeling comfortable and confident to ask questions and request support.

In facilitating these workshops, it became evident in the formal conversations with the participants that when they met other Indigenous HDR students with similar backgrounds, experiences and/or concerns about belonging, that by participating in NIRAKN had helped to reinforce that they do belong in academia.

We also spent time discussing how to navigate academia if the end goal of the participants was to work as an academic.

3.7 Learning How to Play 'The Game'

> [NIRAKN] helped me to understand what is involved in an academic career pathway (WEF_IndigenousHDR5).

Acquiring academic capital also involved talking about how to be an academic and unpacking how academics are evaluated. "Understanding the academic game and how to play it and/or be aware of it" was mentioned by a participant. The information shared relating to this comment included the metrics universities keep on academic staff members, including the number of grants applied for and awarded, the number of students being supervised and the number and quality of publications by academics.

The issue of relationships with supervisors was often raised and is the focus on Chap. 6. However, once we informed students that supervisors are evaluated based on the number of HDR students they have and the rate of completions, this helped the students understand the nature of the reciprocal relationship. By having conversations about the metrics kept on academics, a shift was sensed in how the students understood the relationship with supervisors. They now understood that the relationship was designed to be mutually beneficial. Despite this knowledge, students still tended to report that they felt they were a burden to their supervisors.

We felt it was also important to spend some time discussing what the role of a supervisor entails and what it does not. When students understood what roles belong with the supervisor and what roles reside with the candidate, the boundaries were much clearer (see Chap. 6 for more insight).

Another conversation that emerged was about HDRs being offered co-authorship of publications with academics who had completed research on Indigenous matters. Being asked to co-author a paper was discussed as both an opportunity and a challenge. The opportunity is about obtaining a publication, and the challenges are about providing some form of authority that what has been conducted and/or written involved respectful and/or appropriate means for engagement with Indigenous peoples involved in the research. Another related challenge was about contributing to a publication outside your own discipline and/or the time being a co-author takes away from your own research. Ultimately, the choice resides with the candidate, who needs to weigh up the advantages and disadvantages of being a co-author.

The facilitators were also able to share with the HDR students how as an academic post-PhD they may be invited to be a CI on ARC grant applications where Aboriginal and/or Torres Strait Islander academics are needed. Again, the same challenges as stated above apply, with a further challenge of being limited to being a CI on two ARC discovery applications, thus making it important to be involved in projects connected to your discipline and/or passion and also knowing the other academics involved and making sure you feel that you can work with these individuals.

3.8 Becoming an Academic

> Even though I knew my topic area better than anyone, I was given excellent direction and support from First Nations Peoples who had the right knowledge and experience in areas I was less confident (WEF_IndigenousHDR10).

Aside from networking, NIRAKN was deemed helpful by participants during each stage of the HDR journey. 'Playing the game' of becoming an academic involves completing various milestones for a doctoral thesis. NIRAKN participants commented on the usefulness of NIRAKN during the confirmation, data collection, data analysis, writing up and presentation stage of their journey.

3.8.1 Confirmation

During the confirmation stage, one participant stated that by attending the NIRAKN workshops "[they were] finally reading the right books and learnt about methodologies that made sense" (WEF_IndigenousHDR13). Another participant mentioned that NIRAKN help them to "clarify [their] research topic and research question … [and] scholarly sources to cite … [and] developed [their] critical thinking" (WEF_IndigenousHDR3). Other participants mentioned how attending the workshops helped build their confidence and cultural support, with one stating that NIRAKN "helped [them] to prepare for [their] next steps in [their] PhD and meet others at a similar stage to share ideas" (WEF_IndigenousHDR12).

3.8.2 Data Collection

Participants stated that the data collection stage was helpful because: "It provided me with insight on ethical research approaches and methods. It reminded me of the political and personal reasons of why my research is important and why I am doing it. The conversations about Indigenous research at the workshop helped keep me on track" (WEF_IndigenousHDR3).

Participants often mentioned the political and personal reasons for conducting their research. As facilitators, we often had to redirect statements such as "I'm doing this research for my Community" to "You are doing this research to make a new contribution to knowledge in your discipline". Reminding students what the requirements of a research degree entails helped to reposition the duties and responsibilities back on the candidate.

Another participant mentioned that "I was able to find research methods that suited my mob based on information shared in NIRAKN" (OLS1_IndigenousHDR13). Similarly, another participant stated that NIRAKN "provided information about Indigenous research approaches" (OLS1_IndigenousHDR5) and that the workshops "built my understanding and knowledge of Indigenous research methodologies" (OLS1_IndigenousHDR7). NIRAKN may be the only national workshop that has focused on Indigenous Research Methodologies and Methods for HDR students.

Finally, a participant stated that the workshop "helped me consider other things for my data collection I hadn't thought about" (OLS1_IndigenousHDR12). Here, the participant may have been referring to the discussion that 'you aren't giving back to the Community by conducting research', because the research degree is awarded to the HDR candidate, and all information contained in the thesis belongs to the candidate.

3.8.3 Data Analysis

NIRAKN participants also reported that the workshops helped with the data analysis stage of their candidature. "It helped me interrogate the assumptions behind different analytical frameworks. Although my study had already been designed with an analysis plan developed, it helped me to cast a critical eye over what I was planning to do with the data" (OLS1_IndigenousHDR2).

As HDR students engage in conversations about their milestones, they demonstrate that they do belong and that they have the shared language other academics used in higher education settings. For instance, one participant stated that the NIRAKN workshop "enabled me to think deeply about the theoretical premise of my research, which was critical to my analysis" (OLS1_IndigenousHDR7). Most individuals outside of academia likely do not talk about theoretical frameworks informing their analysis. So, whether participants realised it, being a participant in NIRAKN workshops also involved transitioning from sitting on the sidelines feeding your imposter syndrome to sitting tall and being an academic.

3.8.4 Write Up

Although capacity-building workshops are widely available to all HDR students at universities across Australia, it has been reported that many Indigenous HDR students have not attended these sessions. One participant commented that "I had spent a long time at other universities never having the writing process and thesis structure explained to me. NIRAKN workshops were critical in explaining how my thesis should be structured and supporting me with my academic writing" (OLS1_IndigenousHDR7). In the workshop, we also focused on how theses are examined. Another participant stated that "it was extremely helpful. It was the first time I was introduced to the examination criteria for PhD theses – it helped me to understand the examination criteria and the idea of writing to an audience" (OLS1_IndigenousHDR2).

Citing the works of Indigenous scholars was also discussed as a way to pay respect to the scholars around the world who had laid the foundations for Indigenous scholars and who continue to do so. The importance of acknowledging the work of Indigenous scholars who have come before them was captured by this quote: "I felt that I was on the right path in continuing the work of others that came before me. It gave me a sense of direction" (OLS1_IndigenousHDR13).

Another participant stated that "I was able to recall the Indigenous scholarly sources that I could refer back to and cite" (OLS1_IndigenousHDR3). Another participant recalled the importance of other students sharing their process: "Just hearing other students' experiences and ideas helped me think about mine and prepare" (OLS1_IndigenousHDR12). Providing a space for Indigenous HDR candidate to feel comfortable sharing their progress, strategies and tips also provided benefits to other participants, who were able to see value in what was being shared.

3.8.5 Presentations

The last area participants commented on was in delivering academic presentations. "It's really helped me to gain a better sense of what entails a good research presentation. Not only did the workshop highlight the features of presenting research, but the calibre of the presenters evidenced how to present knowledge and research" (OLS1_IndigenousHDR2). Learning by observing facilitators present at NIRAKN events also demonstrated how to present in an academic setting. Another participant mentioned that the NIRAKN workshops "gave me confidence because I had discussed my research in front of other Indigenous critical thinkers beforehand, and from that I was able to consider the perspectives of others in my research and feel more comfortable when talking with other Indigenous people and others about my research" (OLS1_IndigenousHDR3). Learning how to present and how to take feedback and/or questions from the audience without bringing emotions into the discussion was also seen as a valuable lesson. Making sure that you are comfortable presenting and discussing the topic was deemed an important self-reflection practice to consider before presenting in academic settings.

3.9 The Legacy Phase

During 2021 and into 2022, NIRAKN enters the legacy phase of the project, with funding scheduled to end on 31 December 2022. All the capacity-building resources will be available from the NIRAKN Website (see nirakn.edu.au). Despite the successes of NIRAKN, all good things usually come to an end. As such, we encourage all higher education institutions with Indigenous HDR candidates to invest in professional development to support their candidatures. Insights on how best to do this can be gleaned from the NIRAKN annual reports (see Anderson, 2020).

We also have a cautionary note about how Indigenous HDR students should also be prepared throughout their candidature to be competitive postdoctoral fellows because, despite the focus on the requirements of the HDR candidature, Mantai (2019) argues that doctoral studies are not enough to become an academic. Other considerations are the importance of juggling other academic duties, such as tutoring and/or lecturing, being involved in other research projects and/or offering services to the discipline or community through organising conferences and peer reviewing papers. In the next chapter, we will focus on another key component to being an academic having agency in an academic context.

References

Anderson, P. (2019). *NIRAKN annual report for 2019*. https://www.nirakn.edu.au/
Anderson, P. (2020). *NIRAKN annual report for 2020*. https://www.nirakn.edu.au/
Behrendt, L., Larkin, S., Griew, R., & Kelly, P. (2012). *Review of higher education access and outcomes for Aboriginal and Torres Strait Islander people* (1922125253). Department of Industry, Innovation, Science, Research and Tertiary Education (Australia).
Clance, P. R., & Imes, S. A. (1978). The imposter phenomenon in high achieving women: Dynamics and therapeutic intervention. *Psychotherapy: Theory, Research and Practice, 15*(3), 241–247.
Edwards, C. W. (2019). Overcoming imposter syndrome and stereotype threat: Reconceptualizing the definition of a scholar. *Taboo: The Journal of Culture and Education, 18*(1). https://doi.org/10.31390/taboo.18.1.03
Mantai, L. (2019). 'Feeling more academic now': Doctoral stories of becoming an academic. *Australian Educational Researcher, 46*, 137–153. https://doi.org/10.1007/s13384-018-0283-x
Moreton-Robinson, A. (2016). National Indigenous research knowledges network (NIRAKN)—Some reflections and learnings. *International Journal of Critical Indigenous Studies, 9*(2), 1–9.
Moreton-Robinson, A., Anderson, P., Blue, L. E., Nguyen, L., & Pham, T. (2020). *Report on Indigenous success in higher degree by research*. Australian Government, Department of Education and Training. https://www.qut.edu.au/?a=921040
Wilson, S. (2008). *Research is ceremony: Indigenous research methods*. Fernwood Publishing.

Open Access This chapter is licensed under the terms of the Creative Commons Attribution 4.0 International License (http://creativecommons.org/licenses/by/4.0/), which permits use, sharing, adaptation, distribution and reproduction in any medium or format, as long as you give appropriate credit to the original author(s) and the source, provide a link to the Creative Commons license and indicate if changes were made.

The images or other third party material in this chapter are included in the chapter's Creative Commons license, unless indicated otherwise in a credit line to the material. If material is not included in the chapter's Creative Commons license and your intended use is not permitted by statutory regulation or exceeds the permitted use, you will need to obtain permission directly from the copyright holder.

Chapter 4
The Role of Agency in Higher Education: Acquiring Academic Capital

Abstract Indigenous higher degree by research (HDR) students navigating higher education institutions continue to face additional challenges that are not associated with the research degree they are pursuing. Racism continues to be identified as a barrier present in academic settings and society. The impact of racism may affect an individual's agency and their ability to acquire academic capital. Both agency and academic capital may also influence how an individual is supported throughout their candidature and ultimately become a factor in the success of the HDR student's research degree. In this chapter, we discuss the role of agency and academic capital among Indigenous HDR students and then connect our findings to how Indigenous HDR students ($n = 99$) report that agency and/or how academic capital has influenced their experience in higher education. This chapter is also informed by insights from supervisors of Indigenous HDR students ($n = 33$).

Keywords Agency · Higher education · Indigenous · Academic capital

4.1 Introduction

Many Indigenous higher degree by research (HDR) students have reported having a lack of agency in academia and/or a lack of academic capital (Burgess & Lowe, 2019; Crocker & Robeyns, 2009; Kosko, 2013). By agency, we are referring to the ability to navigate within academia by acquiring the necessary capital (i.e. academic capital) to make this possible (Bourdieu, 1977). We posit that academic capital is similar to identity capital, which is defined as "investments people make in who they are, but these investments can be strategically self-generated" (Côté & Levine, 2014, p. 123). Therefore, by referring to 'academic' capital, we are specifically referring to the investments people make in an academic context; for example, obtaining a degree, membership of scholarly societies and participation in academic committees.

Indigenous HDR students can also have the unfortunate task of navigating through systemic structural barriers or "*structure*, rather than being determined by it" (Amundsen, 2019, p. 426), meaning that there are often more obstacles for Indigenous HDR students or indeed any HDR student who are at risk of being impacted by systemic structural barriers within academia. One of these structural barriers is a lack of agency because Indigenous HDR students are often the first in their family to complete a postgraduate degree (Cameron & Robinson, 2014; Gore et al., 2017; O'Shea et al., 2013). The role of agency is vital to embrace once the decision to enrol in higher degree education is made (Amundsen, 2019). By having agency in a higher education context, HDR students can begin to realise their own worth, act independently and make autonomous choices (Amundsen, 2019; Barker, 2005).

Acquiring agency in the higher education context means that Indigenous HDR students may begin to understand that they have choice about who their supervisors are and choice about the research project they undertake. Understanding how academia works may help to shift the power balance between supervisors and students. For instance, knowing that academics need HDR students to supervise may help HDR student understand that it is also in the best interest of academics to be supervising students. Understanding their role as a HDR student may also help students manage their expectations and encourage them to take responsibility for scheduling meetings and setting agendas, as many supervisors often only provide what they are asked for and may not know whether anything additional is required unless it is specifically requested.

In this chapter, we discuss our findings based on interviews via group discussions and written responses of Indigenous HDR students ($n = 66$) and a survey of supervisors of Indigenous HDR students ($n = 33$) that explored their needs and experiences. We discuss the role of agency in higher education that an Indigenous HDR student might encounter in the following situations when:

- navigating the terrain of academia as an Indigenous HDR student;
- encountering racism in higher education settings;
- the relationship between student and the supervisor fails;
- there is a need to reach out for additional academic support.

In the next section, we discuss the terms 'identity', 'agency', 'culture' and 'capital' to explore their similarities and differences.

4.2 Identity, Agency, Culture and Capital

Amundsen's (2019) research with Māori students in higher education settings found that "transitions to higher education for Māori students involve a reciprocal interplay of identity, agency and structure which support or constrain transition experiences" (p. 426). We are focused on how Indigenous HDR students are supported in higher education settings to succeed. As such, we are interested in the role of agency and identity or identity capital in an academic context, which we refer to as academic capital. Amundsen argues that Māori university students "require agency to articulate their own identity positions, values and beliefs through having a voice" (p. 407). Therefore, cultural identity is also an essential component to consider when thinking about the role an Indigenous HDR students has in an academic setting. "Cultural identity comes about as a result of how individuals define themselves in relation to culture(s) to which they belong – an interaction between self and society" (p. 417).

Cultural identity and cultural capital appear to be linked and may enable and/or constrain an individual's ability to navigate higher education based on how much or how little their culture is valued by the institution. Culture has been previously defined as "symbolic vehicles of meaning, including beliefs, ritual practices, art forms, and ceremonies, as well as informal cultural practices such as language, gossip, stories, and rituals of daily life" (Swidler, 1986, p. 273). Determining whether culture is valued at the university may be ascertained in various ways. For instance, value may be found to be explicit because it is written in the university's blueprints that outline their strategic plans and vision (see Queensland University of Technology [QUT], n.d.-a). Or 'value' may be found in reconciliation action plans, or it may be implicit and stated in informal discipline meetings and/or associations connected to the university. How much your culture is perceived to be valued by the university will likely have an impact on the HDR student's agency in a higher education context.

Barker (2005) believes that 'agency' is better if it is connected to an 'agent–situation interaction', suggesting that is 'done together' rather than individually acquired. Therefore, "instead of agency existing within individuals, agency is shifted to the capacity of the context for action as shaped by the interaction of those individuals in that context" (Amundsen, 2019, p. 372). There is no doubt that the ability to make change, have action and transform practice is dependent on the values held by the university about Indigenous peoples, which demonstrates the power of the 'agent–situation interaction' or context-specific understanding of agency.

The authors of this chapter are all employed by QUT. The values held for Indigenous Australians is explicit and intertwined in everyday practices of the university under Vice-Chancellor (VC) and President of the University Professor Margaret Sheil's leadership. Changes to QUT since VC Sheil's appointment include hiring Angela Barney-Leitch as QUT's first Pro-Vice Chancellor (Indigenous Strategy). Angela was responsible for the 'Campus to Country' initiative (QUT, n.d.-b). The Carumba Institute (QUT, n.d.-c) was established to increase Indigenous Australian research focus, continue to develop Indigenous Australian researchers and to meet the needs of Indigenous Australian students and is led by Executive Director, Professor Peter Anderson. A joint initiative between the Carumba Institute and the QUT Academy of Learning and Teaching (QALT) focuses on embedding Indigenous perspectives in curriculum, which is called Indigenous Learning and Teaching initiatives (QUT, n.d.-d). This initiative provides staff members with professional development to embed Indigenous perspectives in their curriculum. Carumba staff, Professor Anderson and Dr. Levon Blue, have also developed two units for undergraduate students that are being piloted before they become implemented across the university. These units have been designed as independent online units that provide the student with an opportunity to engage with Indigenous perspectives in respectful ways that are supported by a rights-based approach (see Anderson & Rhea, 2018). The above initiatives are only some of the visible changes in practices that QUT has undertaken under Professor Sheil's leadership and her commitment to Indigenous Australians. When core business is aligned with valuing of Indigenous perspectives, it helps to ensure that Indigenous people, including Indigenous HDR students, are valued within QUT.

With Indigenous perspectives valued at QUT, it might be the case that Indigenous HDR students will have agency and/or a better chance at acquiring agency. However, Côté and Levine (2014) write about identity capital resources or assets that also have an impact on an individual's identity and their ability to acquire agency whether context specific or not. Identity capital resources or assets can be both tangible and intangible. The tangible assets are visible by others and include degrees and memberships of academic societies. The intangible assets "involve ego strengths (synthetic and executive) that entail reflexive-agentic capacities such as an internal locus of control, self-esteem, a sense of purpose in life, the ability to self-actualize, and critical thinking abilities" (Côté & Levine, 2014, p. 144).

Thinking about identity capital in both tangible and intangible terms may help to explain why for some individuals acquiring a research degree is not enough to self-actualise into becoming an academic. Understanding identify capital and the complexities often experienced by Indigenous HDR students navigating systemic structural barriers must be considered by the interplay of all the intertwined concepts, including agency, identity, cultural capital and academic capital. It is easier to place blame on the individual for failing to achieve than to understand how the intangible assets are required to "understand and negotiate various social, occupational, and personal obstacles" (Côté & Levine, 2014, p. 145). In addition to these obstacles for Indigenous HDR students, this often involves facing and confronting racism.

Having a voice in a higher education context is not as simple as it might sound. Let us explain. It involves having agency (individual notion and agent–situation interaction that is context specific and dependent) and academic capital, which includes assets that are both tangible and intangible. Therefore, speaking up does not always equate to agency because it is largely dependent on who is speaking up, the environment where the speaking up is happening and the tangible and/or intangible resources of the individual who is speaking up.

4.3 Participants, Data Collection and Analysis

As described in Chap. 1, the participants of this research were Indigenous HDR students enrolled in higher education institutions across Australia. Informing this chapter are datasets 3, 4, 5 and 6, as shown in Table 4.1. Four different forms of data were collected. In 2018, we conducted group interviews and collected written responses from the same 34 participants. We also conducted an online survey in 2020 seeking to understand more about the needs and experiences of Indigenous HDR students ($n = 32$) and supervisors of Indigenous HDR students ($n = 33$). Therefore, a total of 66 Indigenous HDR students and 33 supervisors of Indigenous HDR students have informed this chapter. For more information about the methodological approach and/or the data analysis process, see Chap. 1 (p. 13) and Chap. 3 (p. 46).

4.3 Participants, Data Collection and Analysis

Table 4.1 Datasets used to inform this chapter

Dataset number	Type (written evaluation form, group discussion, written response and/or online survey)	Year collected	What it is and who it includes	Number of participants	Referred to in text as
3	Group discussion (qualitative)	2018	Discussion about needs and experiences of Indigenous HDRs (Indigenous HDRs)	34	GD_IndigenousHDR
4	Individual written responses (qualitative)	2018	Written responses about needs and experiences of Indigenous HDRs (Indigenous HDRs)	34[a]	IWR_IndigenousHDR#
5	Online survey (qualitative and quantitative demographic information)	2020	Survey about the needs and experiences of Indigenous HDRs (Indigenous HDRs)	32	OLS2_IndigenousHDR#
6	Online survey (qualitative and quantitative demographic information)	2020	Survey about the needs and experiences of Indigenous HDR students (supervisors and Indigenous HDR students)	33	OLS3_Supervisor#
Total participants				99	

[a]The same participants who completed the group discussion also provided a written response to additional questions. We only counted these participants once despite their participation being in two different sets of data

4.4 Instances When Agency in a Higher Education Context Might Be Needed

In this section, we discuss four situations when agency might be needed during the HDR degree. The first occurs when navigating higher education as a HDR student. The second is when Indigenous HDR students encounter racism in higher education settings. The third example is about relationships between students and their supervisors and their potential breakdown. The fourth example occurs when Indigenous HDR students need to reach out for additional support relating to research skills.

4.4.1 The Role of Agency Navigating the Terrain of Academia as an Indigenous HDR Student

Universities are keen to increase the number of Indigenous students completing research degrees (Department of Education, 2019). One participant from the group interviews mentioned the importance of explaining what the main purpose of a HDR is when institutions are seeking additional students from varying backgrounds, including from non-traditional pathways:

> HDR is an opportunity for you to demonstrate that you can independently do a body of research. I didn't know that's what an HDR was. I did a PhD because I knew I needed it to be an academic. I did not know that a PhD was literally an example for you to do that because you come in and you get told your supervisors and that they've got power and you have to meet with them and things like that. Until I realised that this was about me demonstrating my ability to do it, I did not know that I had agency to go and do those things (GD_IndigenousHDR).

The participant further described how knowing what their role was as a HDR student meant that they learned to behave differently in academic spaces compared to how they were taught to behave in Community spaces.

> So, trying to recognise how to show respect and when I'm used to working in reciprocal community type spaces, then going, 'Oh, this isn't about me just listening to them like I would to Elders, this is about me actually bringing stuff to the table. Great, I now have the freedom to do that', but I think that's an equity versus equality kind of discussion. It's not about babysitting Aboriginal students. It's about saying that six months that I wasted that I could've been spending time getting published, that other HDR students, the majority of them who come from those wealthier, more elite backgrounds, have used more productively than me because they came in with knowledges that I don't have due to these other factors, but it wouldn't just be Aboriginal students (GD_IndigenousHDR).

The participant from the group interview highlights the insider academic knowledge or academic capital that students with family or friends who have completed research degrees may have access to—knowledge that may help guide the HDR student navigate the space more strategically with regard to publications and opportunities to seek tutoring or research assistant work. The realisation that other HDR

4.4 Instances When Agency in a Higher Education Context … 45

students have published and/or are tutoring and/or are employed on other academic projects as research assistants may come as a surprise to students who are actively building their academic CV while completing their research degree. As the participant shared, "they just need to consider that there are assumed knowledges that aren't there for every student" (GD_IndigenousHDR).

Related to the need to gain academic experience during a research degree, Professor Peter Anderson shared this advice with Indigenous HDR students who participated in the group discussions:

> It's sort of do as I say and not as I did. And don't go into faculty and let them load you up with work that you will not finish, and then your dean comes to you and says, 'You know what, you either have to submit or you lose your job.' And it's as simple as that. So, they get us in and they load you up, so be mindful – and that's your own agency. You choose to take that on, and you choose to be in the faculty, in the academy, but you have to take what comes with it. You either get in or get out, is what I say to my students.

This advice underscores the need for Indigenous HDR students to be in control of their workload and the importance of gaining additional experiences while remembering that completing the research degree is of prime importance.

4.4.2 The Role of Agency When Indigenous HDR Students Encounter Racism in Higher Education Settings

> I don't think any of our institutes of higher education are culturally safe for Aboriginal and Torres Strait Islander students. At the HDR level I have found that even more so. There seems to be added scrutiny and expectation with the racism (OLS3_Supervisor25).

It is not just Indigenous HDR students who notice and mention racism in academia. As stated earlier by a supervisor of an Indigenous HDR student, there is concern about academic institutions being a culturally safe place for Indigenous HDR students. One supervisor elaborated on the racism experienced 'at all levels' throughout academia:

> All HDR students are entering a neoliberal institution and precarious economy. My Indigenous students also deal with tremendous racism at all levels – from peers, academics, institutions and in disciplinary scholarship. I worry I am not as effective as I could be in fighting this. The balance between preparing students for the institution, warning them, and respecting that their experiences and politics may differ a lot from mine is tricky to strike sometimes. Universities need to deal with the extent of the racism and eurocentricity/white supremacism so that the supervision relationship doesn't have to constantly strategise/heal this stuff (OLS3_Supervisor26).

Another supervisor of an Indigenous HDR student echoed the concerns above by focusing on how academia still challenges Indigenous research methodologies and/or methods:

> The academy is not well suited to support Indigenist research, making it challenging for Indigenous students – timelines don't factor in or support true community partnership, Indigenous knowledges and methodologies still questioned etc.; institution needs to have

supports in place (family leave, cultural leave, peer support networks and mentoring etc.) also zero tolerance to racism and better awareness among non-Indigenous scholars about Indigenous scholarship (OLS3_Supervisor22).

This concern was also connected to another comment by a different supervisor about the need for the Graduate Research Centres to adjust their practices, which might be done by having the supports in place as mentioned in the previous quote: "Graduate Research Office – not understanding what it takes to have Indigenous students in HDR. Their timelines are unrealistic and inflexible" (OLS3_Supervisor21).

Indigenous HDR expressed their concerns about racism in higher education in other ways. For instance, this HDR student turned the gaze to supervisor's practices: "Aside from the more obvious concerns such as racism and white supremacy present in the academy, I often worry that there are not enough supervisors who employ culturally sound methods into their practices" (OLS2_IndigenousHDR4).

Another Indigenous HDR student shared their frustration about dealing with white fragility when arguing about systems and structures in place that perpetuate inequalities for Indigenous peoples:

> My biggest concern is receiving drafts of my chapters back with tracked changes that completely change my writing to make it more palpable for a non-Indigenous audience. This isn't something that non-Indigenous students experience. But in my experience, I need to be constantly aware of not offending white sensibilities because my supervisor can take some of my critiques of systems and structures personally and get offended by them (hello white fragility). I wish my supervisor would just step back and realise that this is my thesis – not theirs – and view my arguments for their merit, rather than watering down my arguments because they make my supervisor uncomfortable (OLS2_IndigenousHDR1).

The ability to listen to each other in the student and supervisory relationship is essential. At times, the student is learning from their supervisors and at other times the supervisors may be learning from their students. As another HDR student stated, the belief that you can change unjust practices is important for HDR students:

> If you are someone who is diligent and methodical when it comes to solving different problems or issues then give higher research a go. I don't consider myself the smartest person but I have found a topic I'm passionate about and it has driven me to get the best out of myself particularly because I think my topic could contribute to systemic change for blackfellas (OLS2_IndigenousHDR3).

In order to pursue a passion for a HDR project to work towards systemic change, it is vital to transform unjust systems, structures and practices in academia and replace these with just ways of being, doing and knowing. We would argue that the more an Indigenous HDR student is able to exercise their agency, the greater the likelihood that the student will be able to convincingly argue their position with supervisors and push forward with their progress.

4.4.3 The Role of Agency When the Relationship Between the Indigenous HDR Student and the Supervisor Fails

> One supervisor I had completely ignored me all the time, would not respond to emails and would not address me in a room (while addressing other PhD students). I changed him as a supervisor this year (OLS2_IndigenousHDR21).

As discussed in Chap. 2 (see Sect. 2.3.3), the student–supervisor relationship does not always last the duration of the candidature. Some students might feel locked into the relationship and be uncertain about how to fix the situation:

> I felt shame keeping up with deadlines and shame around my writing. It was paralysing me. Eventually after talking with Elders and other HDR students I got the courage to speak with him. The relationship and the writing got better (OLS2_IndigenousHDR31).

Seeking advice and counselling from others was key to improving the relationship that the Indigenous HDR student previously described. Knowing that you have options and that others have likely navigated something similar may help to ensure the HDR student does not give up:

> My primary supervisor circulated an email saying I was incompetent to the other supervisors and research assistants. This was a blatant act of bullying and not true or helpful in any way. I was forced to report the supervisor for inappropriate behaviour and then rebuild the working relationship without an apology or acknowledgement (OLS2_IndigenousHDR5).

The example quoted here demonstrates that this HDR student knew the relevant policies and reported the supervisor's behaviour. It is conceivable that this supervisor has learned not to behave in this manner despite the student not receiving an apology or an acknowledgement; we argue here that this HDR student used their agency to seek out the appropriate way to report this behaviour:

> … your supervisor allowing you to take responsibility for your studies and giving you the tools to have agency within how you approach your study and being kind of open and receptive to how you work and how they work as well. So, two-way communication I guess for me is really important (GD_IndigenousHDR).

The above quote highlights what a sense of agency about their project may result in. This sense of direction and progression to the end goal seems possible when the HDR student feels like they are supported and encouraged by their supervisor along the way.

4.4.4 The Role of Agency When Indigenous HDR Students Need to Reach Out for Additional Academic Support

> If you think because you are around lots of intelligent and well-intended people that the environment will systematically support you as an Aboriginal academic you might be in for a rude awakening (OLS2_IndigenousHDR24).

This student also mentioned the importance of seeking supervisors with the expertise that are needed in your studies. This could be a supervisor with the theoretical expertise, the methodological expertise and/or the discipline expertise. The need to learn from experts along the way was viewed as an essential part of the research degree. However, Indigenous HDR students also reported situations where they were educating their supervisors about Indigenous ways of conducting research (see Chap. 7 for more details).

> It's really been around educating them [about] Indigenous ways of doing in research, or ways of viewing the world, and having that make them feel deeply uncomfortable to the point where they try to change the way you want to do things. That really stifles your willingness to keep working with someone who just can't critique their assumptions and be open to seeing another way of doing (OLS2_IndigenousHDR1).

An Indigenous HDR student also mentioned the need to be told and/or shown the ropes in academia as there is a lot of academic jargon that is not common knowledge:

> Find an Indigenous group or mentor who can explain or translate a lot of the academic terminology. Have them walk you through study tips, back-up files, and learn what a systematic review is all about. Lockdown is exactly what HDR studies is all about – to some degree (OLS2_IndigenousHDR26).

Comparing completing a research degree to being in lockdown is a timely comparison that illustrates the sense of isolation students can feel throughout their candidature.

4.5 Summary

In this chapter, we shared why and how acquiring agency in a higher education context may contribute to an Indigenous HDR student successful experience completing their research degree. We highlighted the four situations when both Indigenous HDR students and supervisors of Indigenous HDR students mentioned agency might be helpful. These situations included when an Indigenous HDR student navigating academia, when they encountered racism, when their relationship with their supervisor failed and when there was a need to reach out for additional academic support.

References

Amundsen, D. (2019). Student voice and agency for Indigenous Māori students in higher education transitions. *Australian Journal of Adult Learning, 59*(3), 405–434.
Anderson, P. J., & Rhea, Z. M. (2018). Rights-based Indigenous education in Australia: Evidence-based policy to pedagogy. In *Evidence-based learning and teaching* (pp. 205–216). Routledge.
Barker, C. (2005). *Cultural studies: Theory and practice*. Sage.
Bourdieu, P. (1977). *Outline of a theory of practice*. Cambridge University Press.

References

Burgess, C., & Lowe, K. (2019). Aboriginal voices: Social justice and transforming Aboriginal education. In K. Freebody, S. Goodwin, & H. Proctor (Eds.), *Higher education, pedagogy and social justice: Politics and practice* (pp. 97–117). Springer. https://doi.org/10.1007/978-3-030-26484-0_7

Cameron, S., & Robinson, K. (2014). The experiences of Indigenous Australian psychologists at university: Experiences of Indigenous psychologists. *Australian Psychologist, 49*(1), 54–62. https://doi.org/10.1111/ap.12036

Côté, J. E., & Levine, C. G. (2014). *Identity, formation, agency, and culture: A social psychological synthesis*. Psychology Press.

Crocker, D. A., & Robeyns, I. (2009). Capability and agency. In C. W. Morris (Ed.), *Amartya Sen* (pp. 60–90). Cambridge University Press.

Department of Education. (2019). *Indigenous students in higher degrees by research. Statistical report, August 2019*. https://www.dese.gov.au/download/4830/indigenous-students-higher-degrees-research/7202/document/pdf

Gore, J., Patfield, S., Fray, L., Holmes, K., Gruppetta, M., Lloyd, A., Smith, M., & Heath, T. (2017). The participation of Australian Indigenous students in higher education: A scoping review of empirical research, 2000–2016. *The Australian Educational Researcher, 44*(3), 323–355. https://doi.org/10.1007/s13384-017-0236-9

Kosko, S. J. (2013). Agency vulnerability, participation, and the self-determination of Indigenous peoples. *Journal of Global Ethics, 9*(3), 293–310. https://doi.org/10.1080/17449626.2013.818385

O'Shea, S., Harwood, V., Kervin, L., & Humphry, N. (2013). Connection, challenge, and change: The narratives of university students mentoring young Indigenous Australians. *Mentoring & Tutoring: Partnership in Learning, 21*(4), 392–411.

QUT. (n.d.-a). *QUT blueprint 6*. https://cms.qut.edu.au/__data/assets/pdf_file/0006/894066/qut-blueprint-6-final.pdf

QUT. (n.d.-b). *Campus to country positioning strategy*. https://cms.qut.edu.au/__data/assets/pdf_file/0018/1008522/QUT_Campus-To-Country_small.pdf

QUT. (n.d.-c). *Carumba Institute*. https://www.qut.edu.au/research/carumba-institute

QUT. (n.d.-d). *Indigenous learning and teaching perspectives*. https://www.qut.edu.au/news?id=178674

Swidler, A. (1986). Culture in action: Symbols and strategies. *American Sociological Review, 51*, 273–286.

Open Access This chapter is licensed under the terms of the Creative Commons Attribution 4.0 International License (http://creativecommons.org/licenses/by/4.0/), which permits use, sharing, adaptation, distribution and reproduction in any medium or format, as long as you give appropriate credit to the original author(s) and the source, provide a link to the Creative Commons license and indicate if changes were made.

The images or other third party material in this chapter are included in the chapter's Creative Commons license, unless indicated otherwise in a credit line to the material. If material is not included in the chapter's Creative Commons license and your intended use is not permitted by statutory regulation or exceeds the permitted use, you will need to obtain permission directly from the copyright holder.

Chapter 5
Indigenous Higher Degree by Research Students' Needs and Experiences

Abstract This chapter focuses on the needs and experiences of Indigenous higher degree by research (HDR) students in academia. The study employed qualitative research methods, including group discussions and individual written responses ($n = 34$) and an online survey ($n = 32$). The participants were Indigenous HDR students from different disciplinary fields from across Australia who participated in this research during 2018 and 2020. Specifically, this research project explored the students' needs and experiences during their candidature. We found that the role of supervisors in the students' HDR journey impacted their sense of agency and their opportunities for mentorship and networking within their discipline. Indigenous HDR student specifically reported the need for: (1) quality supervision; (2) mentoring opportunities; and (3) access to research training. The reported needs bring the spotlight on how increasing retention rates of Indigenous HDR students might be possible.

Keywords Indigenous · Higher degree by research · Needs · Experiences

5.1 Introduction

Studies over the past decade have identified the low participation rates of Indigenous higher degree by research (HDR) students in higher education. Behrendt et al. (2012) outlined a number of barriers influencing Indigenous HDR students' completion rates, including the need for better supervision. The literature on Indigenous HDR students has tended to focus primarily on culturally appropriate aspects of supervision rather than on the academic skills needed to accomplish a research degree (Barney, 2013; Moodie et al., 2018; Trudgett, 2008).

The participation and retention of Indigenous students have revealed the fact that Indigenous students are largely under-represented in HDR programs in Australia (Barney, 2013; Behrendt et al., 2012). While quality supervision plays a critical role in supporting Indigenous HDR students and enabling them to succeed, there are few studies investigating the association between quality supervision and Indigenous HDR students' needs and practical experiences. Laycock et al. (2009) and Trudgett

(2011, 2013, 2014) have provided practical guides for supervisors to support Indigenous students, including developing and maintaining strong and trusting relationships, and supervisors having respect for students. Recently, Hutchings et al. (2019) suggested training for supervisors in Indigenous research methodologies, and the ethics of working with Indigenous people and communities should be introduced.

5.2 Background

The Australian Government's Department of Education and Training compiles data on the enrolment and employment of HDR students and staff, respectively, at Australian universities. In 2020, Moreton-Robinson et al. completed a commissioned report for the Department of Education and Training. This report on Indigenous success in HDR (see Moreton-Robinson et al., 2020) utilised the Department of Education and Training's data to illustrate and discuss the significant imbalance in the number of Indigenous and non-Indigenous HDR students and staff in Australian academies. In 2017, the data from the Department of Education and Training revealed that there were 592 Indigenous Australians enrolled in a research degree and there had been 60 completions. The number of Indigenous HDR students enrolling or commencing and completing their degrees throughout the years is not equal. We know from the existing data that completion rates continue to be extremely low compared to the number of enrolments and commencements over the preceding years. Although the number of Indigenous students enrolled in a research degree has gradually increased, the number of students who actually commenced their study and completed study fluctuated in this period. For instance, in 2006, there were 357 Indigenous students enrolled in a HDR program, but only 86 (24.1%) Indigenous students actually began their research journey, and only 33 (9.24%) Indigenous students completed their degree. This trend continued in the following years from 2007 to 2017. It is interesting that the number of Indigenous HDR students enrolled in a research degree has increased in the recent years from 2014 to 2017. The number of Indigenous students who completed their research study was highest in 2016.

In comparing the number of HDR students in the total domestic population, the number of Indigenous HDR students is alarmingly low. Even in 2016 when the Indigenous HDR students recorded the highest completion rate, it is only approximately 0.9% of the total domestic population of HDR students.

5.3 Quality Supervision

Indigenous HDR students require high-quality supervision in supporting them to achieve their academic goals (Trudgett, 2008). A strong and trusting supervisor–student relationship is recommended, and Trudgett (2008) also suggests that students need to be respected as knowledge holders. Trudgett (2011) argued that Indigenous candidates may have different supervisory needs from non-Indigenous candidates such as supervisors with cultural awareness and knowledge of Indigenous ancestry and history. The Australian Council of Learned Academies' review of the Australian research and training system states that without adequate Indigenous HDR supervisor training, supervisors may be ill-equipped to acknowledge the merits of Indigenous research methodologies, knowledges and protocols. Thus, quality supervision has been identified as one of the contributing factors that Indigenous students will consider in choosing an institution (Page et al., 2017). Several studies offer practical guides for supervisors of Indigenous research students (e.g. Laycock et al., 2009; Trudgett, 2013, 2014). There are limited number of studies that have focused on the needs and experiences of Indigenous HDR students.

5.4 Supervising Indigenous HDR Students

The impact of supervision on the retention and completion of Indigenous HDR students was investigated by Dunbar et al. (2004) and Laycock et al. (2009). Dunbar et al. (2004) identified that non-Indigenous supervisors might not feel confident in supporting the needs of Indigenous students, which may be different from non-Indigenous students. The authors found that the differences in perspectives and support needs of Indigenous HDR students, Indigenous matters and support and training techniques may disturb and influence the confidence of non-Indigenous supervisors even though they may be experienced research supervisors.

Laycock et al. (2009) indicated the dilemma in incorporating an Indigenous worldview into Western research methodologies and recommended a reciprocal relationship between supervisors and novice researchers to be successful in supporting research activities and drawing on the specialised and complementary expertise of each person. However, these studies failed to discuss whether supervisors' availability and/or workload impacted their support for Indigenous HDR students.

Harrison et al. (2017) discerned that supervisors' knowledge and skills have an impact on students' research development. They emphasised the importance of supervision and recommended that supervisors have an open mind and respect for Indigenous knowledges and ways of doing and respect Indigenous students as knowledge holders. They also focused on supervisors' academic skills and capability to supervise Indigenous research students in a culturally appropriate and safe way. However, it remains unclear how culturally appropriate supervision contributes to the success of Indigenous research students in higher education and what culturally appropriate supervision actually means.

5.5 Participants

The participants in this research study were Indigenous HDR students from different disciplinary backgrounds and universities across Australia. These participants attended capacity-building workshops facilitated by the National Indigenous Research and Knowledge Network (NIRAKN) and participated in an online survey via the Qualtrics platform.

5.5.1 Data Collection

Data collected for this research focused on the needs and experiences of Indigenous HDR students. Four types of data were obtained, as shown in Table 5.1. For a complete list of the datasets informing this book, refer to Chap. 1.

The data from the group discussion (dataset 3) was analysed to understand the needs and experiences of Indigenous HDR students. The data obtained from the individual written responses (dataset 4) was analysed to provide an in-depth understanding of Indigenous HDR students' challenges, experiences of good practices in HDR supervision and suggestions about supervision during their candidature. The individual written responses took 30 min for participants to complete. Data from the online survey that Indigenous HDR students completed (dataset 5) was analysed to understand the needs and experiences of candidates.

5.5.2 Data Analysis on Indigenous HDR Students' Needs and Experiences of Research Supervision

The study adopted a qualitative approach to obtain an in-depth understanding of the needs and experiences of Indigenous HDR students concerning supervision. The qualitative approach offers an effective way for researchers to achieve a comprehensive overview of the study, including the perceptions of the participants (Miles & Huberman, 1994). A qualitative approach was chosen for its advantages and appropriateness to investigate the needs and experiences of supervision of Indigenous research students. The study also involved identifying what Indigenous HDR students considered to be important factors to enable their success as HDR candidates.

Group discussions were recorded, and these audio files were transcribed by a professional transcription service. The process of data analysis in this study consisted of three phases: Phase 1, data screening for its completion, fitness and to obtain a general sense of the data; Phase 2, coding the data into nodes using NVivo; and Phase 3, interpreting the data by reviewing themes that emerged from the nodes.

NVivo Pro 12 software was used to analyse and code the data. The data was coded by tagging text with codes as a way of indexing for easy retrieval in the

5.5 Participants

Table 5.1 Datasets used to inform this chapter

Dataset number	Type (written evaluation form, group discussion, written response and/or online survey)	Year collected	What it is and who it includes	Number of participants	Referred to in text as
3	Group discussion (qualitative)	2018	Discussion about needs and experiences of Indigenous HDRs (Indigenous HDR students)	34	GD_IndigenousHDR
4	Individual written responses (qualitative)	2018	Written responses about needs and experiences of Indigenous HDR students (Indigenous HDR students)	34[a]	IWR_IndigenousHDR#
5	Online survey (qualitative and quantitative demographic information)	2020	Survey about the needs and experiences of Indigenous HDR students (Indigenous HDR students)	32	OLS2_IndigenousHDR#
Total participants				66	

[a]The same participants who completed the group discussion also provided a written response to additional questions. We only counted these participants once despite it being two different sets of data

coding process. To code the passages of text into nodes, a line-by-line analysis was implemented. Each node was carefully examined to understand the data that was coded against the node.

For the purpose of analysis, several themes were identified from each node and sorted into the categories of each of the different datasets. To begin this process, each node was examined in detail. The next step in this process was to reexamine the categories and identify identical themes that were found in most of the nodes and represented the needs and experiences of Indigenous HDR students of supervision. These categories are discussed next.

5.6 What We Need

The findings in relation to Indigenous HDR students' needs and experiences are discussed in this section. Two main categories were found in the group discussion and individual interviews, and a third category was found in the online survey: (1) quality supervision, (2) mentoring opportunities and (3) access to research training.

5.6.1 Students Need Quality Supervision

We found that students expect the following attributes of quality supervisors:

- Sets clear expectations from the beginning
- Devotes time for meetings and supporting students
- Fosters respectful relationships
- Holds discipline and/or methodological expertise.

Relationships between academic supervisors and HDR students can be very complicated, and they may contribute to students exiting early if the relationship encounters challenges. Setting clear expectations and open communication is important for all HDR students. Indigenous HDR students seek to establish these expectations with their supervisors to ensure long-term and cooperative relationships. One participant in a group discussion revealed:

> I think another thing that's really important in a supervisor for me is that they can be upfront about their working style and what they need from you. So, being able to tell you, I [the supervisor] prefer to get an email before you present your writing, or something like that. It's really important for you to know what your supervisor's preferred style is but for them to know what your preferred style of working is and somehow meet in the middle (GD_IndigenousHDR).

Another participant also agreed, stating that "she structures communication, we set clear boundaries" (GD_IndigenousHDR). This finding confirms the matching expectation between Indigenous HDR students and supervisors of Indigenous HDR students in setting clear expectations at the beginning of supervisor–student relationship (see Chap. 6 for details). This finding is also in accord with Cardilini et al. (2021) indicating that "expectations of both candidates and supervisors were closely aligned at the beginning of candidature with both groups placing high importance on qualitative attributes such as candidate motivation, enthusiasm, and written communication" (p. 6).

When asked about the quality of supervision, many of the participants in the group discussion and individual written responses were unanimous in the view that regular meetings greatly contribute to the understanding and efficiency in the supervisor–student working relationship. Whether face-to-face meetings or in-person meetings, it is critical for supporting Indigenous HDR students in completing their research projects. One of the participants stated that "[The supervisors] needs to be committed to meetings and provide support in timely manner" (GD_IndigenousHDR). Another

5.6 What We Need

participant added that they sought "regular meetings every fortnight or monthly so that the supervisors can provide them feedback and support their study" (GD_IndigenousHDR).

The results of this study also revealed that supervisors' availability and commitment to support are critical to Indigenous HDR students. In a group discussion, a participant indicated that they required a lot of support. Another respondent added:

> I also have support from the [name of the unit] Unit. They listened to me. Before I'd even enrolled in the PhD program, they had – my two potential supervisors had an hour chat with me where I just talked around a table like this with just those guys in a room. They devoted an hour of their time. They're both really, really busy on projects – where I could just tell them about my project. So, they suggested people I could read. They were thinking about their own projects and where that could fit into that as well and it was just a totally – being listened to I think for me is a really important part of that and written feedback and support. I need to know that I'm in a safe, supportive environment (GD_IndigenousHDR).

More than half of the students (52%) who participated in the group discussion indicated that supervisors' support was the key factor contributing to the quality of supervision. In response to the question about quality of supervision, one respondent mentioned that they were also seeking support in the research journey and career goal. The findings relating to the Indigenous HDR students' perspectives of quality supervision involving regular meetings and providing feedback and support matched with supervisors' perspectives (see Chap. 6). Understanding the needs of HDR students, particularly Indigenous HDR students, supervisors who participated in this study reported that quality critical feedback is one of the strategies they use. The supervisors also reported that they support their students holistically (i.e. culturally, mentally, personally and academically). This finding is also in line with those of previous studies (Barney, 2013; Behrendt et al., 2012; Schofield et al., 2013; Trudgett, 2011, 2014; Trudgett et al., 2016) with regards to the type of support for Indigenous HDR students.

In line with these findings, Trudgett (2008) recommended four types of support to enable Indigenous HDR students to succeed, including quality supervision, financial assistance, the Indigenous department at their institution and the support provided by the candidate's family and community.

Another Indigenous HDR student added in the individual written response that quality supervision is "when supervisor challenges but supports me as well".

We also found that Indigenous HDR students sought a respectful relationship with their supervisors in an environment where students could be supported by their supervisors. A participant in a group discussion revealed:

> It's got nothing to do with culture and that stuff. I just need to know that I'm safe and I'm supported and the other thing that was great is they were excited and enthusiastic about your project and make you feel like this is worth doing (GD_IndigenousHDR).

Another participant also agreed with this statement and reported that they need supervisors who are "respectful [and seek] quality over quantity supervisors regarding meetings, uplifting (walk with me in my research journey), providing and/or directing towards tools" (GD_IndigenousHDR).

While Trudgett et al. (2016) mentioned age as a factor influencing supervision success, the current study found supervisors' expertise play a crucial role in students' research. When asked about the quality of supervision, the majority of participants in the individual written responses agreed with the statement that they need their supervisors' expertise and professional experience and knowledge in the disciplines. The words 'knowledge' and 'professional' are repeated 24 times in the participants' responses. What is clear from these students' responses is that supervisors must comply with universities' standards for supervision and be experts in their disciplines to enable students to succeed in their research journey.

5.6.2 Supervisors with Expertise and Experience

Two broad themes emerged from the analysis of students' experiences of supervision practices. A variety of perspectives were expressed on the practices of supervisors. The results of this study found both 'good' practices and others that students had concerns about.

'Good' practices of supervisors included possessing scholarly disciplinary knowledge and/or a good understanding of the HDR process. For example, one participant wanted supervisors who had "knowledge of discipline and ability to guide professionally through HDR process" (OLS1_IndigenousHDR33).

Other good practices identified by Indigenous HDR students were respecting students' knowledge and cultures, being available and interested in the student's research and having a reciprocal supervisor–student relationship.

One of the interviewees who commented on respecting students' knowledge and cultures noted:

> I've had a non-Indigenous supervisor who is quite open minded and willing to learn from where I was coming from, where my position was and was willing to shift their understanding. So, we had theoretical debates where we were at odds with each other, and it was a very open, collegial kind of conversation (GD_IndigenousHDR).

Another participant in a written response added that "I had a supervisor who accepted my weird ideas and went away to read about it and we discuss" (GD_IndigenousHDR).

These findings may point to a lack of knowledge about Indigenous research methodology held by HDR supervisors. Prior studies (Martin, 2003; Nakata, 1998; Rigney, 2011; Trudgett, 2014; Trudgett et al., 2016) have also argued the importance of Indigenous students' voices by creating an intellectual space that acknowledges Indigenous students as respected knowledge holders of, for example, a specific Indigenous research methodology. We also note that being Indigenous does not equate with using Indigenous research methodologies (see Chap. 7), nor does every Indigenous HDR student carry Indigenous knowledges that are relevant to their HDR studies.

5.6 What We Need

When asked about good practice of supervisors, several interviewees agreed with the statement that supervisors' understanding of the HDR process is critical. An Indigenous HDR student stated that their supervisors "need[ed] to have knowledge of the institution and what academia is, the administration, the process of HDR and that sort of stuff" (GD_IndigenousHDR). Another participant believed that supervisors need to:

> focus on four elements: (1) Pastoral care for the student (i.e., emotional support); (2) Research support/advice/supervision (i.e., specifically related to the project, advice about conducting thematic analysis); (3) Establishing deadlines and other motivators to enable the research to keep progressing; (4) Critical reflection for both the student and the supervisor (i.e., challenges our assumptions, knowledges and ways of doing) (OLS2_IndigenousHDR1).

Trudgett (2014) emphasised the critical role of regular meetings in supporting students to succeed. Commenting on the availability of supervisors, another Indigenous HDR student reported that they were seeking supervisors who were approachable, engaged and would give feedback on their work.

As mentioned above, Indigenous HDR students considered the supervisors' availability and interests in students' research as a primary factor of supervisory quality. For instance, one student said "We don't meet often because they're leaders in their field but they make time for me and when they do make the time, even if it is every two and a half months" (GD_IndigenousHDR). Another Indigenous HDR student wrote:

> I have a good professional relationship with my supervisors. I like that she is available at any time for me. I can email, text, pick up the phone and call. He will always answer. That flexibility is important to me because I have two young children, and my PhD moves around this (GD_IndigenousHDR).

These responses reflect those of Trudgett (2014), who also found that a strong relationship between supervisors and students is critical to the accomplishment of Indigenous Australian doctoral students. This view was echoed by another Indigenous HDR student who believed that the reciprocal relationship between supervisors and HDR students was a good practice.

> I think relationships between supervisors is also important. It's been important for me. Two of my supervisors, non-Indigenous, they have a pretty good success rate of pushing PhD students through, including Indigenous students. So, they work really well together – good cop, bad cop. So, when we're in a meeting together, but also behind the scenes – they have critical discussions about my work and about what they should be giving, and that's been effective, I think (GD_IndigenousHDR).

While many good practices were reported in the individual written responses and shared in group discussion, students had other concerns about supervision practices, including forcing students to conduct studies in the area of supervisors' interests, supervisors' lack of disciplinary knowledge and supervision expertise and supervisors' unavailability to meet and provide feedback for students.

Regarding research conducted in the area of supervisors' interests, an Indigenous HDR student said "when a primary and secondary supervisor strongly advise you to do a particular research in a way other than your thought – because it would be good for that faculty to have done that study" (GD_IndigenousHDR).

Another participant was also dealing with the same issue and stated that "my ideas are irrelevant and I should follow her [supervisor's] ideas and do what she does in her practice" (GD_IndigenousHDR).

Participants also mentioned that supervisors' lack of knowledge of a specific discipline and/or supervision expertise was the main reason for their concerns. In one case, a participant in a group discussion described an unprofessional and unexperienced supervisor in the supervisory team:

> That was my point about that they [supervisors] need to know the systems and processes because I had – not really similar situations but I had a supervisor at a previous university that had only just done a master's and should never have been supervising and didn't know anything. So, actually being a proper supervisor and knowing that stuff is important (GD_IndigenousHDR).

Inexperienced and unprofessional supervisors were reported to cause problems when they try to direct or lead the research area without any expertise or previous experience and with a demonstrated incapacity in the topic area of the student. Another participant stated that ideal supervisors are:

> Supervisors who know and have experienced the content and life experiences of their HDR students. Supervisors who know the administration procedures of their own university. Supervisors who can direct HDR students to the appropriate contact to find the correct information. Supervisors who don't seem to be 'winging it' and learning how to support HDR students as they go (OLS2_IndigenousHDR6).

The most obvious finding to emerge from the analysis is that the supervisors' unprofessional expertise causes numerous problems and concerns for HDR students. What we can discern from the above comments is that unprofessional expertise strongly influences on building trust and respect in the supervisor–student relationship, concerning students' sceptical thinking on leading supervisors. Our study confirms that Indigenous HDR students expect their supervisors to have discipline expertise and experience in the academy (see Chap. 6).

5.6.3 Mentoring Opportunities

Indigenous HDR students also mentioned the role they believe their supervisors play in providing mentorship during their candidature.

> Quality supervision is to build up the capacity of the student to undertake independent research by providing a supportive, enthusiastic and positive environment. Ideally, the supervisor will be able to provide guidance to benefit the student in areas of methods development, research and data processing in addition to opportunities for leadership, personal and academic growth (OLS2_IndigenousHDR10).

5.6 What We Need

Another student mentioned the important role supervisors play in helping their students navigate the space since they are experienced and have a better idea what opportunities exist.

> I just expect guidance and feedback mainly because this is all new to me, and they have done this before and had other students they know what to do. It would be quite difficult I would imagine trying to do a PhD on your own without anyone providing feedback or saying it think you should include this, or do that (OLS2_IndigenousHDR34).

The role of supervisor is thought to include mentorship by sharing the unknown formula of achieving HDR completion.

> I expect support, encouragement, knowledge and experience of the academy and institutional processes. I expect this because it should be like a mentor relationship, and also because they are like a 'teacher' for the formula of how HDR works (OLS2_IndigenousHDR9).

According to Lindén et al. (2013) "mentoring is supposed to involve more personal, intimate, pastoral relations, besides interaction relevant to the student's professional socialisation, whereas advising is restricted to questions concerning research tasks" (p. 640). Mentoring programs are independent and separated program from supervision and not regulated at national level, but at faculty level (Lindén et al., 2013).

Knowing how to provide career advice about being an academic was also viewed as valuable. For students seeking a job in academia post their HDR, the role of building a competitive CV during their candidature is important.

> Guidance, feedback and a listening ear when I have a challenge in my work. It would be great if they offered advice as to a future career or advice on publishing academic papers, what conferences to attend etc. to further my career (OLS2_IndigenousHDR17).

Another student suggested that supervisors should provide opportunities to their students using their own research programs. However, this suggestion could open up difficult situations if the supervisor role was responsible for both the completion of students' HDR milestones and employment duties. Instead, supervisors could recommend opportunities they hear about from other academics rather than employing their own student.

> I think my supervisors are interested in the topic and more broadly self-determination. Constructive feedback they are encouraging and identify where I need to improve. Promote opportunity with more broadly across the university through their networks. Use their own research accounts to provide me further opportunities (OLS2_IndigenousHDR24).

In addition to mentoring opportunities, Indigenous HDR students also mentioned the importance of having access to research training.

5.6.4 Access to Research Training

Not all HDR students start their research degree directly after completing an undergraduate degree with an honours component. Many Indigenous HDR students mentioned the need for research training during their candidature.

> I had a big break between Honours and PhD – on returning for the post-grad degree, there was minimal interrogation of my ability to do the research and the Confirmation process was therefore pretty chaotic. In hindsight, I should have been started in a Masters by Research in order to gain some detailed research skills. I think the excitement of getting an Aboriginal post-grad in the school played a small part in this. Gotta love hindsight … (OLS2_IndigenousHDR19).

Another Indigenous HDR student mentioned the formal research training they completed.

> I completed the Professional Certificate in Indigenous Research at the University of Melbourne and helped me greatly in many ways, from explaining and delivering that explanation of my research to others, especially those outside of my field (OLS2_IndigenousHDR22).

This Indigenous HDR student reflected on the capacity-building training they received through the National Indigenous Research and Knowledges Network (NIRAKN; see Chap. 3 for more information about NIRAKN) and the impact it had on them.

> In my first year I attended a few NIRAKN events. These were invaluable in exposing me to some of the challenges that lay ahead. Presenting at the ANU Indigenous research symposium was a great experience. This level of critical analysis of my work (by the best) provided me with the motivation to keep going (OLS2_IndigenousHDR27).

Another Indigenous HDR student mentioned how they are actively seeking research training during their candidature that "I have to actively go out and find training but all things related to research methodologies and technologies that expedite research processes are the most helpful" (OLS2_IndigenousHDR30).

The value of research training was captured by another Indigenous HDR student who shared how they can take knowledge away from any training and make it applicable to their circumstances.

> I can learn from any training, I can bend it, shape it, deconstruct and reconstruct, but I acknowledge that much research training overlooks Aboriginal research approaches, exiting expertise, practices and aspirations, researching training from Indigenous knowledge systems better suit my needs for development, delivered by Aboriginal researchers for us and our communities (OLS2_IndigenousHDR7).

The need for training on Indigenous research methodologies and research practices was echoed by another Indigenous HDR who was seeking to share their traditional knowledge and practices with other Indigenous HDRs. They highlighted that many of the challenges and/or struggles Indigenous HDRs are wrestling with now existed years ago.

> As a prospective Elder in community I have always had a keen interest in Ancestral Intellect. In mainstream education and knowledge is kept to the 'young'. The 'young at heart' like me want to share my learned skills with community members who want to develop proactive interests in research and parallel them with Ancestral Intellect. Our mob think they are learning new things, however a lot of these issues were around back in the days of the Ancestors. We just have forgotten most of it (OLS2_IndigenousHDR26).

The findings about Indigenous HDR students' needs for accessing research training are consistent with other studies that report research training is essential (Barney, 2016; Behrendt et al., 2012; McGagh et al., 2016; Moreton-Robinson et al., 2020). The importance of offering research training to Indigenous HDRs in both Indigenous approaches and Western approaches to research was requested by many Indigenous HDR candidates.

5.7 Summary

The current study was designed to explore Indigenous HDR students' needs and experiences to understand what is needed to succeed in their research degree. The study employed a qualitative method using group discussion, individual written responses to collect data and an online survey. Sixty-six Indigenous HDR students in different disciplinary industries from across Australia participated in this research. The study revealed that building a respectful supervisor–student relationship and being supervised by supervisors with the appropriate discipline knowledge are vital for the success of Indigenous HDR students as the supervisors' expertise, professional experience and knowledge in the disciplines are primary academic mechanisms in enabling Indigenous HDR students to succeed. Indigenous HDR students also identified the important role supervisors play in providing mentoring during their candidate and the need for access to research training. With completion rates of Indigenous HDR students lagging behind non-Indigenous HDR candidates, it may be timely to reevaluate the roles supervisors play in their success and provide targeted ways for active mentorship and access to research training throughout their research degrees.

References

Barney, K. (2013). 'Taking your mob with you': Giving voice to the experiences of Indigenous Australian postgraduate students. *Higher Education Research & Development, 32,* 515–528.

Barney, K. (2016). Pathways to postgraduate study for Indigenous Australian students: Enhancing the transition to higher degrees by research. Australian Government. https://altf.org/wp-content/uploads/2016/08/Barney_NTF_Report_2016.pdf

Behrendt, L., Larkin, S., Griew, R., & Kelly, P. (2012). *Review of higher education access and outcomes for Aboriginal and Torres Strait Islander people* (1922125253). Department of Industry, Innovation, Science, Research and Tertiary Education (Australia).

Cardilini, A. P. A., Risely, A., & Richardson, M. F. (2021). Supervising the PhD: Identifying common mismatches in expectations between candidate and supervisor to improve research training outcomes. *Higher Education Research & Development,* 1–15. https://doi.org/10.1080/07294360.2021.1874887

Dunbar, T., Arnott, A., Scrimgeour, M., Henry, J., & Murakami-Gold, L. (2004). *Working towards change in Indigenous health research* (CRCAH research report) (p. 68). Cooperative Research Centre for Aboriginal and Tropical Health.

Harrison, N., Trudgett, M., & Page, S. (2017). The dissertation examination: Identifying critical factors in the success of Indigenous Australian doctoral students. *Assessment & Evaluation in Higher Education, 42*, 115–127.

Hutchings, K., Bainbridge, R., Bodle, K., & Miller, A. (2019). Determinants of attraction, retention and completion for Aboriginal and Torres Strait Islander higher degree research students: A systematic review to inform future research directions. *Research in Higher Education, 60*(2), 245–272. https://doi.org/10.1007/s11162-018-9511-5

Laycock, A., Walker, D., Harrison, N., & Brands, J. (2009). *Supporting Indigenous researchers: A practical guide for supervisors*. The Lowitja Institute.

Lindén, J., Ohlin, M., & Brodin, E. M. (2013). Mentorship, supervision and learning experience in PhD education. *Studies in Higher Education, 38*(5), 639–662. https://doi.org/10.1080/03075079.2011.596526

Martin, K. (2003). Ways of knowing, ways of being and ways of doing: A theoretical framework and methods for Indigenous research and indigenist research. *Journal of Australian Studies, 27*(6), 203–214.

McGagh, J., Marsh, H., Western, M., Thomas, P., Hastings, A., Mihailova, M., & Wenham, M. (2016). *Review of Australia's research training system*. https://acola.org/wp-content/uploads/2018/08/saf13-review-research-training-system-report.pdf

Miles, M. B., & Huberman, A. M. (1994). *Qualitative data analysis: An expanded sourcebook*. Sage.

Moodie, N., Ewen, S., McLeod, J., & Platania-Phung, C. (2018). Indigenous graduate research students in Australia: A critical review of the research. *Higher Education Research and Development, 37*(4), 805–820.

Moreton-Robinson, A., Anderson, P., Blue, L., Nguyen, L., & Pham, T. (2020). *Report on Indigenous success in higher degree by research: Prepared for Australian Government Department of Education and Training*. https://eprints.qut.edu.au/199805/

Nakata, M. (1998). Anthropological texts and Indigenous standpoints. *Australian Aboriginal Studies, 2*, 3–12.

Page, S., Trudgett, M., & Sullivan, C. (2017). Past, present and future: Acknowledging Indigenous achievement and aspiration in higher education. *HERDSA Review of Higher Education, 4*, 29–51.

Rigney, L. I. (2011). Indigenous higher education reform and Indigenous knowledges. *Review of Indigenous Higher Education Consultancy*. http://Docs.education.gov.au/system/files/doc/other/rigney_2011.doc

Schofield, T., O'Brien, R., & Gilroy, J. (2013). Indigenous higher education: Overcoming barriers to participation in research higher degree programs. *Australian Aboriginal Studies, 2*, 13–28.

Trudgett, M. (2008). *An investigation into the support provided to Indigenous postgraduate students in Australia* [Unpublished doctoral thesis]. University of New England.

Trudgett, M. (2011). Western places, academic spaces and Indigenous faces: Supervising Indigenous Australian postgraduate students. *Teaching in Higher Education, 16*(4), 389–399.

Trudgett, M. (2013). Stop, collaborate and listen: A guide to seeding success for Indigenous higher degree research students. In R. Craven (Ed.), *Diversity in higher education: Seeding success in Indigenous Australian higher education* (Vol. 14, pp. 137–155). Emerald Publishing.

Trudgett, M. (2014). Supervision provided to Indigenous Australian doctoral students: A black and white issue. *Higher Education Research & Development, 33*, 1035–1048.

Trudgett, M., Page, S., & Harrison, N. (2016). Brilliant minds: A snapshot of successful Indigenous Australian doctoral students. *The Australian Journal of Indigenous Education, 45*(1), 707–709.

References

Open Access This chapter is licensed under the terms of the Creative Commons Attribution 4.0 International License (http://creativecommons.org/licenses/by/4.0/), which permits use, sharing, adaptation, distribution and reproduction in any medium or format, as long as you give appropriate credit to the original author(s) and the source, provide a link to the Creative Commons license and indicate if changes were made.

The images or other third party material in this chapter are included in the chapter's Creative Commons license, unless indicated otherwise in a credit line to the material. If material is not included in the chapter's Creative Commons license and your intended use is not permitted by statutory regulation or exceeds the permitted use, you will need to obtain permission directly from the copyright holder.

Chapter 6
The Needs and Experiences of Supervisors of Indigenous Higher Degree by Research Students

Abstract Supervision is a significant influence in higher degree by research (HDR) students' success. Quality supervision provided to Indigenous HDR students has recently attracted the interest of researchers. This chapter provides an overview of the needs and experiences of supervisors of Indigenous HDR students. We surveyed 33 supervisors to understand their needs and experiences when supervising Indigenous HDR candidates. The perceptions of quality supervision, the good practices and concerns of supervisors and professional development required in supervising Indigenous HDR students were brought to the supervisors who participated in our research. Our study found that it is the mental health and well-being of Indigenous HDR students that raises concerns for their supervisors, while racism is still prevalent. Keeping Indigenous HDR students motivated, being on track and supporting Indigenous HDR students physically, mentally and academically were other concerns found in this study. Specifically, what supervisors of Indigenous HDR students can provide and what they need to best support their students discloses their good practices and concerns in supervision.

Keywords Higher degree by research students · Indigenous · Professional development · Quality supervision · Research · Supervisors · Supervision

6.1 Introduction

The number of Indigenous postgraduate students who enrol in higher degrees by research (HDR) programs has increased 89% since 2005 (Universities Australia, 2020). However, despite the growth in the enrolments in recent years, the completion rates of Indigenous postgraduate research students remain low, and only 0.84% or 54 Indigenous HDR students completed their study in 2018 (Universities Australia, 2020). The disparity between Indigenous and non-Indigenous participation and completion rates for degree qualification is apparent in Australian higher education (Australian Government Department of Education, 2019; Moreton-Robinson et al., 2020; Trudgett, 2011; Universities Australia, 2020). As Trudgett (2011) suggested, "in order for parity to be realized, completion rates of Indigenous doctoral students need to be increased, it is essential that ways to redress such disparity are understood and actioned" (p. 389). There is a growing body of literature that recognises the important role of supervision in supporting Indigenous HDR students in completing their research study (Anderson et al., 2021; Cardilini et al., 2021; Harrison et al., 2017; Hutchings et al., 2018; Trudgett, 2014). However, the research to date has tended to focus on Indigenous HDR students' needs and experiences to better support them holistically and guide them to degree completion (see Chap. 5 for details). Surprisingly, the needs and experiences of supervisors of Indigenous HDR students have not been closely examined.

This chapter presents the findings from our research, which sought to explore the needs and experiences of supervisors in supervising Indigenous HDR students, to better support Indigenous HDR students. In this chapter, the perceptions of quality supervision from the perspectives of supervisors of Indigenous HDR students will be revealed. We also discuss the good practices and concerns when supervising Indigenous HDR students. In addition, the required professional development for supervisors of Indigenous HDR to enable students to successfully complete their research project will be reported.

6.1.1 Supervising Indigenous HDR Students

Indigenous HDR students are distinct from undergraduates in the university system (Hutchings et al., 2019), and supervising Indigenous HDR students requires supervisors to appreciate and learn about Indigenous knowledge and cultural understanding in addition to their expertise. Several lines of evidence suggest that supervisors of Indigenous HDR students can experience the issue of insufficient Indigenous methodologies and/or cultural knowledge (Grant & McKinley, 2011; Hutchings et al., 2019); and "problems can emerge in the relationship between Indigenous HDR students and supervisors when this relationship is overlaid with cultural difference" (Trudgett, 2011, p. 389). As discussed earlier in Chap. 5, a good rapport in the Indigenous student–supervisor relationship strongly supports Indigenous HDR students and is a key factor that contributes to the success of HDR students in completing their research degree. However, building a good rapport in the Indigenous HDR student–supervisor relationship is a reciprocal process: both supervisors and students have to build this relationship cooperatively based on trust and respect since they are not only in the relationship of supervisors and students, but also in the partnership of a long research journey.

In her research of supervision, Trudgett (2011) reported that 47% of participants in her study believed that Indigenous supervision is extremely important. Unfortunately, it would be an impossible and unreasonable task for every Indigenous HDR student to be supervised by an Indigenous supervisor, due to the lack of Indigenous supervisors in Australian higher education. Hence, it is critical to enhance the supervisory development (Henry, 2007; Wilson, 2017) and training of supervisors (both Indigenous and non-Indigenous supervisors; Trudgett, 2011) to better prepare them to work with and supervise Indigenous HDR students.

6.1 Introduction

Supervising Indigenous HDR students requires supervisors to be advocates for their Indigenous candidates, while also reinforcing the motivation and passion of the HDR candidates for their selected research topic (Henry, 2007). Henry (2007) also suggested that supervisors need to be strategic in guiding their HDR students on the journey towards successful completion and that they should develop their Indigenous knowledge, understanding and connectedness, thereby strengthen their relationship with the student as a cultural resource person of high value. However, cultural responsibility and fear of cultural alienation are a unique feature that can potentially impact the success of Indigenous students (Henry, 2007). Therefore, supervisors of Indigenous HDR students must be aware of these issues and be prepared to respond and provide appropriate direction to available resources to assist in finding resolutions (Henry, 2007). Furthermore, Trudgett (2011) recommended that cultural awareness training should be introduced to supervisors of Indigenous students as such awareness can be critical for Indigenous students to achieve their best results.

6.1.2 Roles and Responsibilities of Supervisors

The literature on supervision of Indigenous HDR students has highlighted several responsibilities of researchers in the role of supervisors. Supervisors of Indigenous HDR students not only play the role of a research guide who provides guidance to students and accompanies them in their research journey, but they also have ethical responsibilities, including awareness of Indigenous studies, Indigenous methodologies and Indigenous communities. Furthermore, supervisors have a responsibility to strengthen their supervisory skills by participating in supervision development and cultural awareness training workshops to best support research students, particularly Indigenous HDR students.

It is obvious that guidance is one of the responsibilities of supervisors in higher education. Cardilini et al. (2021) state that "supervisors have a strong responsibility to give guidance and feedback on critical thinking, written communication, and relevant discipline knowledge" (p. 11). However, students in Cardilini et al.'s study also expected supervisors to provide more guidance on developing academic independence, collaboration skills and to maintain motivation. The literature has reported that HDR students who are actively supported and guided to increase their academic independence and collaboration skills will likely have positive effects on their motivation and productivity as well as assist them to develop independent ideas and teamwork skills (Lariviere, 2012; Sinclair et al., 2014).

Supervising Indigenous HDR students additionally requires supervisors to maintain an ethical responsibility "to ensure that the research they [Indigenous HDR students] undertake is beneficial to the Indigenous community and the knowledge they produce reflects accurately local Indigenous worldview" (Wilson, 2017, p. 262). According to Wilson (2017), it is essential for supervisors to have a critical understanding of the past and contemporary context regarding socio-political and historical aspects that have influenced Indigenous communities. Furthermore, supervising Indigenous students who use Indigenous methodologies in the Indigenous community context demands that supervisors have cultural knowledge and cultural awareness of these complex issues (Durie, 2004; Trudgett, 2014).

A growing body of literature has focused on the awareness of the cultural safety and cultural knowledge for supervisors of Indigenous HDR students (Barney, 2016; Behrendt et al., 2012; Durie, 2004; Hutchings et al., 2018; Moreton-Robinson et al., 2020; Trudgett, 2011, 2014); it was found that it is vital for supervisors to participate in cultural awareness training to best support Indigenous HDR students. Also, it is the universities' responsibility to offer cultural awareness training for supervisors. Trudgett (2014) suggested that cultural awareness training should be mandatory to university academic staff and supervisors of Indigenous students "to create a better environment where students feel culturally safe and understood" (p. 1043). Therefore, it is also a responsibility of supervisors to enhance their supervision skills and knowledge by participating in cultural awareness training.

6.2 Methodology

This chapter focuses on the data regarding supervisors of Indigenous HDR students who have experience in supervising these students (i.e. PhD, EdD and/or Master's by research students) at an Australian university and/or higher education institution. An online survey via Qualtrics platform was developed by the authors to collect this data.

Using university networks via email, 33 participants who were supervisors of Indigenous HDR students were recruited from across Australia (see Table 6.1).

Table 6.1 Dataset used to inform this chapter

Dataset number	Type (written evaluation form, group discussion, written response and/or online survey)	Year collected	What it is and who it includes	Number of participants	Referred to in text as
6	Online survey (qualitative and quantitative demographic information)	2020	Survey about the needs and experiences of Indigenous HDR students (supervisors and Indigenous HDR students)	33	OLS3_Supervisor#
Total participants				33	

All of the participants had experience in supervising at least one Indigenous HDR student or were currently supervising Indigenous HDR students. This research focused on seeking to understand supervisors' perceptions of quality supervision and the experiences of supervising Indigenous HDR students, including opportunities and challenges they may face during the supervision process.

The survey comprised demographic questions about participants' ethnicity (i.e. Indigenous or non-Indigenous), highest qualification, years of experience in supervision role, experience of supervising Indigenous HDR students and eight open-ended questions asking participants to share their experience about quality supervision and/or experience with Indigenous HDR students. In the open-ended questions, we also asked participants what professional development is required for supervisors to ensure successful completion of Indigenous HDR students.

Data was analysed using NVivo software. All data uploaded into NVivo will then be coded to identify themes. Once the themes are identified, the data will then be compared to what is reported in the literature.

This qualitative research employed a thematic analysis using NVivo Pro 12 software to analyse data. The open-ended responses collected from the online survey via Qualtrics platform were coded into nodes to identify the themes. The nodes consisted of the questions we asked supervisors of Indigenous HDR students in the online survey. A line-by-line analysis was undertaken to code the passages of text to one or many nodes. Each code was viewed to understand the data that resides with it. The next step involved adding themes about experience and needs of HDR supervisors.

6.3 Results

In this section, we discuss the findings from the online survey in relation to the quality supervision from the perspectives of supervisors and the experiences of supervisors of Indigenous HDR students in the following categories:

- The results from the demographic questions
- Quality supervision from supervisors' perspectives
- Good practices and concerns in supervision
- Professional development for supervisors of Indigenous HDR students.

6.3.1 Demographic Questions

Thirty-three supervisors answered the survey on quality supervision. Of these, 21.2% supervisors were identified as Indigenous people (including Aboriginal and Torres Strait Islanders, Aboriginal and/or Torres Strait Islanders) and 78.8% were non-Indigenous people. A screening question in our survey asked participants whether they had supervised an Indigenous HDR student before to proceed with the next questions. The results showed that 100% supervisors ($n = 33$) who participated in this research had experience in supervising Indigenous HDR students.

The qualifications and experiences of supervisors are important factors in supervising HDR students. The highest qualifications of the supervisors who participated in this survey were doctoral degrees. Of the 33 supervisors, only one possessed a master's degree (3%); 32 participants (97%) possessed a PhD/EdD as their highest qualification. In response to the question about experiences in supervising HDR students, over half of those surveyed (53.1%—17 participants) reported that they had more than 10 years' experience in supervision, 25% (8 participants) had 5–9 years, 15.6% (5 participants) had 1–3 years and only 6.3% (2 participants) had less than one year of experience in the supervision role.

Formal training for researchers in the supervision role is critical for supporting HDR students; also, the experience of supervising Indigenous HDR students was a key point of this study. Of the 33 supervisors who participated in this study, 26 (78.6%) had attended formal training for supervisors and 7 (21.7%) had never attended formal training for supervisors. When asked whether they were currently supervising any Indigenous HDR students, most of the supervisors (93.9%—31 participants) reported that they currently had Indigenous HDR student(s) under their supervision; only two supervisors (6.1%) had previously supervised an Indigenous HDR student, but were not at the present time. We also asked whether the participants had ever supervised a HDR student who was not in their discipline. Interestingly, the results showed that 45.5% (15 participants) said 'yes' and 54.6% (18 participants) said 'no' to this question.

Supervisors' availability for meetings and consultations with students is vital in supervision and critical for working with HDR students. Respondents were asked to indicate the frequency of meeting with students; 21.2% (7 participants) reported that they met with students once a week, 24.2% (8 participants) met once per fortnight, 30.3% (10 participants) met once a month, and 24.2% (8 participants) said that they met with students when needed. In this survey, we also asked participants about the time they spent on supervising an Indigenous HDR student and a non-Indigenous HDR student; the majority of participants (66.8%—22 participants) commented that they spent about the same time for both Indigenous and non-Indigenous students. While 21.2% (7 participants) reported that Indigenous HDR students needed more supervision time than non-Indigenous students, only 12.1% (4 participants) indicated an opposite result that Indigenous HDR students needed less supervision time than non-Indigenous cohorts.

6.3.2 Quality Supervision from Supervisors' Perspectives

Quality supervision plays a vital role in supporting HDR students' success in completing their research degree. This research study focused on the quality supervision from the perspectives of supervisors of Indigenous HDR students. We found that there are a wide range of factors that contribute to quality supervision, including characteristics of the supervisors, supervisors' expertise and experience, quality feedback and advice, the communication and collaboration with students, the student–supervisor relationship, and most of all was the support for Indigenous HDR students holistically.

6.3.2.1 Characteristics of Good Supervisors

> Being flexible if students need more time but rescheduling so that they don't fall of the radar (OSL3_Supervisor27).

A common view among participants about the characteristics of good supervisors was understanding and flexible. As OSL3_Supervisor27 stated above, they [supervisors] are usually flexible in working with students since they also understand that research students have to deal with a range of issues, including family and community responsibilities, work duties and research-related issues. Therefore, "being flexible when students encountered personal and professional challenges" (OLS3_Supervisor12) is a characteristic of supervisors of HDR students, particularly Indigenous HDR students. Another participant commented that [good supervisors] are "supervisors [who] know why and try to understand students' personal and professional situations and help the students to resolve any issue arisen" (OLS3_Supervisor14). Also, to fully understand students, it is critical for supervisors "to listen and really hear what is being asked" (OLS3_Supervisor25) and "listen to what students needs and concerns", as OLS3_Supervisor10 added.

6.3.2.2 Expertise, Experienced and Knowledgeable

Supervisors' expertise in the disciplines, experiences and knowledge is considered to be key factors of good supervision. A recurrent theme in the open-ended responses was a sense among participants that quality supervision comprises supervisors who are knowledgeable, highly experienced and expert in their research area. For instance, a participant said, "expertise in the discipline on the part of the supervisor. Ability to ask pointed questions of students to move them towards a quality research outcome" (OLS3_Supervisor16). Another participant commented:

> [Good supervisors] know the field, have scholarship in the field, have methodological expertise that can support the student, have good ethical understanding and demonstrate it, know of Aboriginal and Torres Strait Islander peoples' protocols, understand the importance of 'talking up' the research with more than just the student (i.e. their community group, employers, especially if they work in the university setting), working with external supervisor partners to make up the expertise that non-Indigenous supervisor don't have (OLS3_Supervisor27).

For supervisors of Indigenous HDR students, knowledge of Indigenous communities and ethical understanding is highly recommended, as Supervisor27 indicated above. Throughout the responses in our data concerning quality supervision, 'knowledge', 'expertise' and 'experience', particularly for Indigenous issues and topics, were repeated multiple times. The following comment illustrates the importance of supervisors' experience:

> Being able to guide and facilitate the student's research. Setting reasonable deadlines and goals. Being able to discuss issues of content (theory, design, results) and process (doing research, doing a PhD) in a meaningful and helpful way (OLS3_Supervisor20).

Another participant stated that experienced supervisors should be able to anticipate examiners' critiques so that they can prepare their HDR students well for the submission of their theses. In particular, one said, "anticipating examiner critique so that the submitted document is as 'bullet-proof' as possible" (OLS_Supervisor12). The same supervisor also pointed out, "helping the student identify the 'ah ha' moment in which they will see the importance of their work". It is apparent that these examples describe the traits of experienced supervisors. However, this study also found a clear message from participants in a supervisory team that inexperienced supervisors who lack the relevant knowledge and expertise should not be placed in the team. A respondent stated:

> Many supervisors – including Indigenous supervisors – have very limited understanding of critical Indigenous research methodologies. Indigenous supervisors are placed on HDR supervisory teams without necessary skills and simply to have an Indigenous person on the panel and Indigenous potential supervisors feel obliged to do so (OLS3_Supervisor30).

In the same vein, another participant added:

> It varies greatly. Many supervisors do not have training in supervision, nor do they seek it out. What is concerning is that non-Indigenous and some Indigenous supervisors see that they can supervise Indigenous students in Indigenous methodology and Indigenous methods even when they have no experience in this or their own research, including their PhDs have not included this at all … There are also people who have not grown up as Aboriginal and/or Torres Strait Islander people or who may have only just learned about their identity in the last few years who think they know about Indigenous knowledge and Indigenous research, Indigenous methodology, Indigenous methods, Indigenous experiences and much, much more. In reality their knowledge is relatively new, just like that of non-Indigenous people. It irks me that people can just be Aboriginal in 1–5 or even 10 years and suddenly they know everything, sit on committees, boards and supervise other Aboriginal people (OLS3_Supervisor30).

6.3.2.3 Quality Feedback and Advice

In supervising HDR students, supervisors' feedback is extremely critical. A word frequency query was run in NVivo software and found that the word 'feedback' was repeated 28 times throughout our data. From the perspective of supervisors, participants indicated the importance of quality feedback in supervision: "Being able to provide quality feedback. Being able to judge the merit of the research and how it will be received by markers" (OLS3_Supervisor20).

"Frequent and timely feedback, able to provide quality feedback, realistic and honest feedback to written work, available at short notice if in a crisis but remain positive, constructive feedback" were other comments recorded in our survey results when we asked participants about quality supervision. Furthermore, a respondent also said: "My job is to give advice where necessary but to not crowd the person so they can fly" (OLS3_Supervisor25).

Obviously, students expect a lot of advice from their supervisors; hence, providing good quality advice strongly influences students' research journey and success. For example, a participant illustrated this point: "My students expect from me a lot of advice on processes, publications, where to find resources, how to manage them, and keeping track of their deadlines for them" (OLS3_Supervisor24).

6.3.2.4 Collaboration and Communication

"Successful and effective supervision requires equal commitment and effort by student and supervisor. This can be hard to achieve" (OLS3_Supervisor24). Some felt that the HDR students' thesis is an individual research project that is assumed to be the responsibility of HDR students only, while our research found that supervisors of HDR students believed that there is an equal commitment and effort by supervisors and students. On that basis, OLS3_Supervisor8 reported that they were working for a common goal. Supervisors of HDR students also wanted to "ensure that HDR students are part of the whole team and not put somewhere separate to the research team" (OLS3_Supervisor29).

Communication is key in successful quality supervision. It was suggested that "setting up a communications process which allows an open and respectful exchange of views on how well goals are being met on both sides" (OLS3_Supervisor24).

It was apparent that communication between supervisors and students requires a respectful exchange of views from both sides. In addition, "constant communication/quick turnaround, regular communication and support, clear communication of objectives, availability and openness, being responsive in communication" were also found in the quality supervision from the perspectives of supervisors.

6.3.2.5 Supervisor–Student Relationship

> In my view it is important to have a genuine rapport between the supervisor and the student and to be interested and concerned both for their well-being, their studies and their future plans. Also to be truthful and honest is key to working together (OLS3_Supervisor8).

Building a good rapport is also key in the supervisor–student relationship. As OLS3_Supervisor8 stated above, it is not only students who are inspired to build a good relationship with their supervisors, but supervisors of HDR students also believed that genuine rapport is important. In addition, trust and respect in this mutual relationship are highly regarded, as noted by one participant: "A trusting and respectful professional relationship with students" (OLS3_Supervisor29). Another participant added: "A respectful relationship, and open relationship where no issues are avoided" (OLS3_Supervisor31).

Additionally, OLS3_Supervisor5 commented that "trust and rapport are essential to this, as is prior experience in working in Indigenous contexts". Furthermore, quality supervision in the supervisor–student relationship also involved "creating relationship with them [students] professionally and personally" (OLS3_Supervisor21) and "ideally, the supervisor-student relationship turns into one of peers over the course of the candidacy" (OLS3_Supervisor1).

Furthermore, "a commitment to a long-term intellectually engaged relationship" (OLS_Supervisor11) is highly recommended, and "having a supportive relationship with students that encourages them to strive" (OLS3_Supervisor17) was highlighted in the responses of quality supervision. Talking about the support for Indigenous HDR students, our study found a range of support from the perspective of supervisors, which will be reported in the next section.

6.3.2.6 Supporting Indigenous HDR Students

Building a strong supervisory team to guide Indigenous HDR students to completion is a vital factor contributing to quality supervision. Once the supervision does not meet students' needs and problems arise, it is the supervisor's responsibility to make students aware of their right to request a reconfiguration of supervisory team, as OLS3_Supervisor27 reported: "making students aware of their right to (re)configure the supervision if it is not meeting their needs". This study also found that supervisors of Indigenous HDR students had a desire to bring a qualified Indigenous supervisor on board to co-supervise Indigenous HDR students and support students from Indigenous supervisors' perspectives. One participant "has tried to bring Indigenous supervisors onto the team where they can support the student" (OLS3_Supervisor27). Although it is not mandatory to include an Indigenous supervisor in the supervisory team for each Indigenous HDR student (see Chap. 7 for more details), involving qualified Indigenous supervisors may better support Indigenous HDR students in their research journey.

Supporting Indigenous HDR students holistically and guiding them to successful completion were found in supervisors' perspectives. This view was echoed by a participant who said they were "supporting the student to complete a project that they are proud of and meets their goals. Guiding the student to completion and examination in a timely manner" (OLS3_Supervisor12).

Additionally, these participants also mentioned that supervisors' support would not cease at students' completion; rather, the supervisors were focused on supporting Indigenous students during the entire process and mentoring for a future career, not just for the degree, but "being a mentor rather than being an authority or absent" (OLS3_Supervisor19). "A highly supportive supervisor would also assist students by creating and maintaining good quality work, enabling high quality work, and ensuring the student has every opportunity to succeed, including the removal of any institutional barriers" (OLS_Supervisor4, 5, 6, 10).

This study also found that supervisors of Indigenous HDR students supported their students by empowering students and challenging them in a supportive and encouraging way to ignite their capabilities and passion for their research project; for instance, a respondent said "supervision that challenges students, holds them to high expectations, but in a supportive and encouraging way, not an overwhelming way" (OLS_Supervisor10). Another respondent added: "Guidance that empowers students to engage with body of knowledge to generate new understanding" (OLS3_Supervisor15).

In our investigation of quality supervision for supporting Indigenous HDR students, we found that supervisors tended to support their students academically, physically, mentally and personally. We also found that students felt safe around supervisors who shared their concerns and interests. The following comments illustrated this perspective:

> The students are adequately supported academically, physically, mentally. Students feel safe around the supervisors, can share their concerns, worries, needs and preferences (OLS3_Supervisor14).

> Having students feel they can discuss any issues with you and working through personality differences. Having students who are passionate about the topic they are researching (OLS3_Supervisor29).

6.3.3 Good Practices and Concerns in Supervising HDR Students

6.3.3.1 Good Practices

Being flexible, understanding and empathetic. A supervisor is who understands life circumstances that may impact their students and their work and who listens to students' interests, needs and concerns that are considered good practices of the participants in this study. Being flexible and empathetic to the students' personal, financial, work-related and study-related situations were also good practices found in this study that are a great support for HDR students; for instance, a respondent said:

> Being flexible as the project changed, as creative practice projects often do. Being empathetic to the situation (personal, financial, work, study) that the student is in, which often changes pretty dramatically over the 3 or 4 years of the doctorate (OLS3_Supervisor6).

Another respondent also checked with students about their care responsibilities and other commitments; this respondent stated:

> I check with students about care responsibilities, partner commitments etc. This helps us get a picture of building this for their lives, setting up goals that are realistic, planning and making it feel more possible. I find younger people who have less community commitments and who don't have children need more help with the planning and juggling. Those who are older with these commitments are used to meeting a range of priorities, commitments and obligations (OLS_Supervisor32).

The good practice of 'understanding' from the perspectives of supervisors of Indigenous HDR students can be identified in various areas, including understanding students' circumstances, context and broader life space issues and when students need assistance or space to think and understanding the issues that may impact students in completing their research project.

Supporting and enabling HDR students to succeed. Bringing Indigenous supervisor into the supervisory team is a great support for Indigenous HDR students. The best option is to have an Indigenous supervisor involved; otherwise, an Indigenous critical friend or other informal mechanisms of Indigenous guidance would strongly support Indigenous students culturally. Furthermore, the findings of this study that confirmed good practices in supervision to support Indigenous HDR students could include a range of strategies such as supervisors' guidance, trainings, feedback, cohort support, expectations and a good supervisor–student relationship.

Providing support and letting students know that they (i.e. supervisors) are here to support them are another good practice that participants in this study have followed. This can be done by regular checking in with students to keep them on track, engage in their research project and talk them through any blockages to find work arounds. In addition, supervisors did not practise micro-managing students' project progress, but encouraged students' independence and skill development. Supervisors were also able to direct students to appropriate support services or courses. For instance, a participant stated:

> I try to check in with my students regularly to let them know I am here to support them. I know that some students retreat and hide when they are feeling overwhelmed or like, they are not doing well, and I try to take that stigma away for them, so they know they can talk to me if they are struggling (OLS3_Supervisor10).

Another respondent stated:

> Providing guidance when necessary and encouraging independence, increasing the independence over time. Encouraging learning (via workshops, training) to improve skill sets. Showing compassion and care when needed. Looking out for opportunities for student development and knowing when to refer on (OLS3_Supervisor13).

According to a participant who had more than 10 years of experience in the role of a supervisor and was currently supervising four HDR students, cohort support is a good practice this participant has followed because that "cohort of students going through the process together, also making sure that they [HDR students] support each other" are opportunities HDR students learn from their cohorts (OLS3_Supervisor23).

Enabling students to succeed in completing their research project requires supervisors to provide critical and timely feedback for their students. Eight out of 33 participants in this study said constant feedback on students' written work was one of the good practices in supervision; for example, a respondent stated "constant feedback on results to bring them to high level of quality research" (OLS3_Supervisor16). Another respondent added: "I provide instant feedback on written material and meet with students to discuss the feedback" to help with "practical matters as they arise, help with writing by commenting on material rather than setting up examples"

6.3 Results 79

(OLS3_Supervisor30, 31). However, "focusing on positives and how work can be improved to give students confidence in their abilities" is another feedback strategy that OLS_Supervisor17 has followed. To enable students' success, a respondent said:

> I think supervisors need to be creative in finding ways of enabling a candidature and making the experience of the student a positive one. I think supervisors need to be proactive in a respectful way to enable the student to succeed (OLS3_Supervisor4).

In this research, we also found that discussing supervisors' expectations with HDR students at the beginning of their research journey is an effective strategy of cooperation for a long-term relationship. Clear expectations were also found to be a good practice in supporting Indigenous HDR students. The term 'clear expectation' was repeated multiple times in this survey's responses. Specifically, a respondent stated "setting out clear expectation for both student and supervisor" had been practised (OLS3_Supervisor21). Also, OLS3_Supervisor26 added: "I like to chat early about expectations, the fact that I've got limits and will stuff up, and talk about ways we can raise and hopefully address stresses or conflicts". In addition to the findings about the clear expectations at the beginning of the research journey, the findings on what supervisors expect from their HDR students will be the focus on further research.

In investigating good practices in supervision that the research participants had followed, the study found that building a reciprocal and respectful relationship between supervisors and students was one in which both supervisors and students bring knowledge and expertise into the supervision space. A participant indicated "the joy of learning new knowledge with students who become experts in their field" (OLS3_Supervisor15). In one case, the participant thought that they did not believe in the student–supervisor relationship, rather they usually learned from each other. Another participant stated that "if they [HDR students] found the supervisor-student relationship isn't helping. I [supervisor] will work with them to find other options" (OLS3_Supervisor26).

Overall, good practices in supervision were found in providing guidance, encouraging students in training for skill development, encouraging cohort support, providing timely feedback, setting up clear expectations and building a respectful supervisor–student relationship. Other good practices were also found in the ways supervisors communicated and cooperated with students to achieve their common goal, which will be reported in the next section.

Communication and cooperation with students. Communication is key in building a good rapport in the supervisor–student relationship and is also key in effective cooperation with students who are working on a project as a team. Communication and cooperation with students regarding frequency of their meetings and time issues were good practices found in this study.

In many cases, participants reported that they were very responsive to students either via emails or phone calls. Several respondents said "students could contact them any time via emails or phone calls and messages as they tried to share up-to-date information with students" (OLS3_Supervisor14). Another respondent also "put students onto custom email lists to get the university announcements and insider information". Particularly, an Indigenous supervisor said "Whanaungatanga, quick response to students, random phone calls outside scheduled supervision to check-in, tautoko – turning up when they are presenting on their work" was their communication style with students (OLS3_Supervisor28). In discussing cooperation with students, one respondent said:

> I work with the student to 'draw' the various part of the project on a diagram and make connections. I find that visualising a project, or at least the methodology section, helps to clarify the mind and makes the writing flow (OLS3_Supervisor12).

Other examples of supervisor–student cooperation to work as a team and target a common goal of completing their research project successfully were noted: "students were also treated as integral members of the whole team" and "reading a shared library on Slack or Google Drive, sharing exemplars". Spending time with students, setting timeframes for students and working towards time issues such as milestone submissions and publications were also critical factors in HDR students' research project. However, the most important thing was giving students time to work on their project and being flexible when students needed more time on it. For example, one respondent reported:

> I set timeframes, I work with students in setting out the timelines to monthly and weekly goals and then even what an average day might look like. This is important in the beginning when they are just getting started and might be unsure. We work together in this process, and put in things like fitness time, picking up kids if they have kids, birthday parties, etc., etc. We look at what community committees and community boards they are on, and how many meetings they can miss a year with an apology and look at being an apology around confirmation time etc. This helps minimise stress at peak times (OLS3_Supervisor32).

As reported in the demographic questions section above, the frequency of meetings between supervisors and students could vary depending on students' needs and the agreement between supervisors and students. The findings in this section also revealed several tips and 'rules' in their meetings. In one case, a respondent said "setting up regular meeting time is the key, and don't cancel the meeting without 24-hour notice". Before a meeting, one respondent usually required students of "work submission for review at least three days in advance". These were task-oriented meetings, and after the meeting, the respondent said that the students were required to email an overview of what had been discussed and a timeline for their next meeting. Another participant stated: "setting feasible meeting time and making sure that other university work does not get in the way of those dates" (OLS3_Supervisor12).

Overall, communication and cooperation with students as a team are practices followed by participants in this study. The communication and cooperation approach revealed effective working styles that have been employed in the supervisor–student relationship. Also, regular meetings to support students in a timely way were highlighted in this finding.

6.3.3.2 Concerns

There were three main issues raised by supervisors concerning their supervision of Indigenous HDR students. The findings of this study found: (1) issues relating to institutions; (2) issues relating to HDR students; (3) issues relating to supervisors.

Issues relating to institutions. When the question "What are your concerns when supervising HDR students?" was put to supervisors of Indigenous HDR students, the responses highlighted the issue of racism and cultural safety in Australian institutions. Several respondents shared the view that Indigenous HDR students have tolerated racism from their peers, academics, institutions and in disciplinary scholarship. The OLS3_Supervisor25 believed that Australian institutions were not culturally safe for Aboriginal and Torres Strait Islander students and that this was more evident at the HDR level.

Another respondent shared a concern that they might not be effective in fighting the racism issue when "all HDR students are entering a neoliberal institution and precarious economy". This respondent also concerned "the balance between preparing, warning students for the institution and respecting for experiences politics which is tricky to strike sometimes" (OLS3_Supervisor26).

Furthermore, OLS3_Supervisor22 believed that "the academy is not well suited to Indigenist research, making it challenging for Indigenous students" and suggested that the "institution needs to have zero tolerance to racism and better awareness among non-Indigenous scholars about Indigenous scholarship".

Additionally, one participant raised attention to the lack support from the Graduate Research Office due to their lack of understanding about the hardship in recruiting Indigenous students in HDR programs. This respondent also claimed their timelines were unrealistic and inflexible. Respondents in this study were also concerned about the insufficient financial support for Indigenous HDR students, which may cause students to withdraw from their HDR programs.

Issues relating to HDR students. Students' mental health and well-being were one of the concerns of the respondents. Pursuing a research degree is a long journey with many up and down feelings and unexpected events that might happen in the students' lives. For instance, a participant said:

> Because it's a long journey and because usually many unintended events happen in the students' lives, some Indigenous HDR students struggle to continue even though they are genuinely interested to continue their studies. So, my main concern is whether the students will actually continue or not (OLS3_Supervisor14).

Other participants expressed their concerns about the mental health of students and the stress of being afraid of failure to complete, "especially not being sufficiently aware of their problems" (OLS3_Supervisor31). For Indigenous HDR students, the burden of family and community responsibilities can affect their study focus and cause poor health and mental issue, which was also a concern of respondents in this study. One participant reported their concern was whether students would be able to complete a task, "especially if they have additional personal demands such as poor health or looking after relatives/community commitments" (OLS3_Supervisor20). Another respondent commented "the students' stress levels and ability to complete their work in a timely fashion to a sufficient standard" (OLS_Supervisor17) was a concern, "especially when they have to deal with the inevitable stress level HDR students experience, particularly with challenging timelines" (OLS3_Supervisor29). Commenting on the stress level and mental health issue of HDR students, another participant said: "mental health of the students as the project creates unique stress in students' life" (OLS3_Supervisor11). Generally, mental health, well-being and stress levels were concerns when supervising HDR students, especially Indigenous HDR students.

"How to keep students on track? How to keep students motivated and interested in the work?" were additional concerns of supervisors. Understanding that the research study is a long learning journey, "whilst the excitement at the initial stages may be contagious, the likelihood of students losing interest is normal. How do we keep students on task and on time?" OLS3_Supervisor15 said. Another said: "From time to time students have difficulty usually related to competing demands on their time which affects progress and can adversely influence work quality" (OLS3_Supervisor18). Furthermore, "the workload model for research supervision is insufficient to help students, so the supervisors get frazzled or don't give enough support for their students" (OLS3_Supervisor27). Expressing a concern when students get behind, this respondent said:

> I think that non-Indigenous supervisors (and I am one) are afraid to ask what is going on when a student gets behind. They [supervisors] need to keep students on track – that's their job … finding out what supports are best to keep them [students] on track. Not being part of a student's community means that there are many things that supervisors are unaware of and they have to work hard to earn the trust and to get into the loop (OLS3_Supervisor27).

However, in contrast to the concerns of supervisors who try to keep students on track, some students do not put their whole heart into their research project, but may treat it as something they do when they have more time and then rush through it at the end. One respondent said:

> Students who treat it [thesis] half-hearted despite saying it's for community and rushing it. It can cause issues in that the work is not as good as it could have been and it has gone too quickly for community too. Sometimes this will come back on the HDR student (OLS3_Supervisor32).

Issues relating to supervisors of HDR students. There were two issues relating to supervisors of Indigenous HDR students that were of concern, including (1) supervisory expertise and (2) alignment with students' expectation.

In many cases, the respondents revealed that they were worried if they were out of depth in relation to theoretical aspects as they wanted to ensure that "students have the breadth of their expertise" (OLS3_Supervisor6). This study also found in the responses that participants were concerned whether "the advice they gave was the best advice", and also, "whether they [supervisors] are doing the good enough job? Whether students feel they are approachable and students can discuss concerns with them [supervisors]" (OLS3_Supervisor23).

In addition to the concern about the depth of expertise to ensure students are being provided with the best supervisory expertise and advice, the participants in this study also reported a concern regarding the alignment with students' expectations. When asked about their concerns when supervising HDR students, one respondent said: "Not being aligned with them [students] in term of expectations. Not being able to help them out properly with ideas" (OLS3_Supervisor19).

Generally, the concerns in supervision were reported in three main issues relating to institutions, HDR students and supervisors of HDR students. In the next section, the findings of this study will report on the professional development for supervisors of Indigenous HDR students.

6.3.4 Professional Development for Supervisors of Indigenous HDR Students

Turning now to the findings of professional development for supervisors of Indigenous students, this section reports the following demands for professional development that will support academic researchers when supervising Indigenous HDR students: (1) professional development in cultural awareness, cultural safety and cultural knowledge training; (2) professional development in HDR supervision and Indigenous research methodology training; (3) professional development in identifying racism and dealing with racism training.

To investigate the demands of professional development to support supervisors in the supervisory role, we asked whether supervisors of Indigenous HDR students required any professional development. The results showed that supervisors of Indigenous HDR students highly valued the importance of cultural awareness, cultural safety and cultural knowledge training. While one respondent said "cultural awareness training is essential", other respondents added:

> It would be good to learn more about dynamics of relationships where one person (supervisor) is more in a position of power. How can we lead and guide but still honour cultural mores, be respectful etc.? I guess that's more cultural training (OLS3_Supervisor10)?

> My practices have been informed by informal conversations with Indigenous colleagues and the families of Indigenous students. I think that there could be some assistance with understanding ways in which Indigenous cultures structure knowledge so that western expectations are not unnecessarily placed on students (OLS3_Supervisor12).

> Cultural understanding. Understanding about Indigenous Ways of Working. Having a clear understanding of the true Australian history. The supervisor needs to be flexible and should be able to work with the students appropriate to their situation. Cross-cultural understanding, understanding about 'cultural safety' is critical. Supervisors need to understand how their behaviour can impact on students' progress (OLS3_Supervisor14).

The participants in this study strongly believed that 'cultural awareness' training is always important in the academy. It would be a great resource for non-Indigenous supervisors and/or supervisors without Indigenous background to learn more "knowledge on culture and perceptions to be able to mentor students better" (OLS3_Supervisor19). Besides, it is critical for Indigenous HDR students to be culturally safe, and including an Indigenous co-supervisor into the supervisory team was suggested as a solution to support Indigenous HDR students. A participant said: "I would love them [students] to have an Indigenous supervisor available to them" (OLS3_Supervisor28). Another participant expressed their perspective on professional development:

> I think all supervisors of Indigenous students should have very careful training; including exposure to basic cultural awareness training, cultural competence training and more intensive training about cultural safety. I think they should be able to demonstrate an understanding of Indigenous Australian epistemology and ontology and understand their own power and privilege as well as their own positionality (OLS3_Supervisor25).

Indeed, supervising Indigenous HDR students requires supervisors' understanding of students' cultural background, understanding of socio-historical landscape to work with Indigenous HDR students and understanding of the needs of HDR students and their motivations for engaging in higher degree. Hence, HDR supervision training is critical for preparing supervisors to do their job well; for instance, one respondent said:

> I do think supervisors require professional development in relation to supervising Indigenous students. Most fundamentally they need other ways to think beyond the dominant deficit discourse of 'needy' students. Part of this is about ensuring supervisors have an understanding of the sociohistorical landscape of their own discipline. This would not only help in supervising Indigenous students, but also help in a broader quest to decolonize academia (OLS3_Supervisor5).

Another respondent stated:

> Supervisors need to learn how to be truly reflective and reflexive in relation to the types of activities that we do as supervisors. While supervisors might have training and learning from other areas of education, it's important that those capabilities are built upon and developed for the particularity of supervision (OLS3_Supervisor4).

While the Indigenous Research Centre has supervisor training workshops, several participants commented that networking opportunities with other supervisors of Indigenous HDR candidates across faculties or meeting with other Indigenous scholars and students to talk about Indigenous research methodologies (OLS3_Supervisor22, 27) were also a part of professional development. In addition, supervisors of Indigenous HDR students should attend Indigenous research methodologies training to understand the protocols for conducting Indigenous research, including Indigenous worldviews and decolonising methodologies (OLS3_Supervisor15). Furthermore, OLS3_Supervisor27 also believed that non-Indigenous supervisors could engage with Indigenous scholarship in a more formal way. Sharing the same view about training for non-Indigenous supervisors, a respondent said: "I would expect that non-Indigenous supervisors of Indigenous HDR students that are undertaking Indigenous research or choosing to operationalise Indigenous methodologies should be provided with professional development to understand critical Indigenous methodologies" (OLS3_Supervisor30). An informant in this study also revealed that learning about Indigenous perspectives, successful approaches to supervision and respect for Indigenous ways of doing and being were important for their professional development.

While racism is still prevalent in Australian higher education and Indigenous HDR students continue to tolerate it, it is important for supervisors of Indigenous HDR students to identify racism and to have the skills and experience to deal with it. Therefore, professional development and training in identifying racism and dealing with racism were reported to be essential. A respondent said: "Training in identifying racism in universities (structural and functional, not implicit bias nonsense) … Procedures for dealing with racism at the university, appeal processes at Graduate School/faculty level" (OLS3_Supervisor26). Additionally, decolonisation and/or antiracism training were found to be recommended in the responses of this study when asked about professional development required for supervisors of Indigenous HDR students.

Overall, the findings of this study highlighted three main issues that require professional development for supervisors: cultural awareness, cultural safety and cultural knowledge training; professional development in HDR supervision and Indigenous research methodology training and professional development in identifying racism and dealing with racism training.

Together, these results provide an important insight into the needs and experiences of supervisors of Indigenous HDR students. This section has presented results from demographic questions and findings about quality supervision from the perspectives of supervisors, as well as good practices and concerns in supervision and professional development required for supervisors of Indigenous HDR. The next section will discuss these results.

6.4 Discussion

This study explored the needs and experiences of supervisors of Indigenous HDR students with an aim to better support Indigenous HDR students and enable them to succeed in completing their research degree project. Drawing from the findings of this study, this section discusses what supervisors of Indigenous HDR students provide (experiences) and what supervisors of Indigenous HDR students need (needs) to provide an understanding about supervisors' perspectives in supervision.

6.4.1 Supervisors of Indigenous HDR Students' Experiences: Quality Supervision

Prior studies have noted the importance of quality supervision in enabling Indigenous HDR students to succeed (Behrendt et al., 2012; Hutchings et al., 2019; Laycock et al., 2009; Moreton-Robinson et al., 2020; Trudgett, 2011, 2013, 2014). The findings of this study highlighted the importance of supervisors' disciplinary expertise, experience and knowledge as a vital factor in quality supervision. It is even more critical to involve a qualified Indigenous supervisor in the supervisory team. These findings are in line with Coopes (2007) and Trudgett's (2011) suggestions "to involve Indigenous community member and elders in the supervision process and incorporate their expertise" (p. 395).

However, as presented in the demographic questions results and as reported by Grant and McKinley (2011), when Indigenous supervisors are asked to work outside their discipline and/or areas of expertise to supervise Indigenous students, there is the perception that Indigenous students need to be supervised by Indigenous peoples, but we would argue that is a myth (see Chap. 7 for more detail). Indigenous students may need support and mentoring from Indigenous people in their community such as from Elders. Here at QUT, the Carumba Institute has an Indigenous Postgraduate Program Officer to provide student support, but not necessarily supervision. The literature seems to support this view that involving an Indigenous supervisor in the supervisory team to act as a cultural advisor and/or associate supervisor is critical for Indigenous HDR students (Anderson et al., 2021; Moreton-Robinson et al., 2020; Trudgett, 2011; see Chaps. 2 and 5). The supervisors' desire to include Indigenous members or elders from the community into the supervisory team is also aligned with Indigenous HDR students' wish to have at least an Indigenous associate supervisor to provide advice and support when needed. Other than supporting Indigenous HDR students culturally, a supervisor's disciplinary expertise is meant to support students to become effective researchers in the academy, and any supervisor should be able to do this well.

Providing quality feedback and advice and building a good rapport in the relationship with HDR students were recorded in quality supervision from the perspectives of supervisors. These findings are consistent with Trudgett's (2014) framework that "providing constructive criticism that is open and honest is academic skill-based support from supervisor and prioritize the relationship with the student (develop rapport) is personal reflection of supervisor" (p. 1046). Furthermore, it is interesting to find the agreement regarding the quality of supervision from the perspectives of supervisors and the perspectives of Indigenous HDR students. As stated in Chap. 1, our study explored the needs and experiences of Indigenous HDR students (see Chap. 5) and the needs and experiences of supervisors of Indigenous HDR students. It is critical to provide an understanding of the same issue from both stakeholders' perspectives. Thanks to this finding, the relationship between Indigenous HDR students and their supervisors might be developed in a positive way. Their cooperation might be more productive and effective for working together as a team for a common goal of completing the research program. Both supervisors and Indigenous HDR students may be more flexible and empathetic in their working relationship when they understand more about students' perspectives and vice versa.

The results of this study showed that quality supervision is also comprised of holistic support for Indigenous HDR students to empower and challenge them in an encouraging way. This is not only about supporting Indigenous HDR students to succeed in completing their research degree, but also to support students personally, physically and mentally during their candidature, as well as in their future academic career. This finding is consistent with the observation that "Indigenous HDR students need a lot of support from their supervisors. Beside the academic support, Indigenous HDR students also expect supervisors' support for their mental health and well-being during their candidature" (Anderson et al., 2021, p. 8). A possible explanation for this finding may be based on the relationship between supervisors and their students. A relationship is built on trust and reciprocal respect. Both supervisors and students have a certain understanding about their counterpart in this relationship. In the role of supervisor, participants in this study understood the students' need for being supported more than anyone. Thus, providing support for Indigenous HDR students holistically to enable their success was not a surprising finding in this study.

6.4.2 Supervisors of Indigenous HDR Students' Needs: Professional Development

The results of this study indicated that supervisors of Indigenous HDR students required cultural awareness, cultural safety and cultural knowledge training to best support their Indigenous HDR students. It is believed that being a supervisor of Indigenous HDR students, an understanding of students' background, cultures, political, socio-historical and economy is critical in guiding Indigenous HDR students. This finding is in agreement with those obtained by Wilson (2017) that "researchers and supervisors of student research have an ethical responsibility to ensure that the research they undertake is (a) beneficial to the Indigenous community and (b) that the knowledge they produce reflects accurately local Indigenous worldview" (p. 262). This finding also confirms Trudgett's (2011, 2014) recommendations about the mandatory cultural awareness training for academics in Australian higher education. This result might be explained by the fact that non-Indigenous and Indigenous supervisors with limited cultural knowledge background experienced challenges and understood their restriction in cultural knowledge when supervising Indigenous HDR students. Therefore, a professional development in cultural awareness, cultural safety and knowledge training is a great support for their supervisory role and responsibilities.

An important finding of this study indicated that supervisors of Indigenous HDR students had concerns about the prevalence of racism in Australian higher education. Showing a concern about racism issues and challenges, Indigenous students have experienced stimulated supervisors' interest in professional development such as workshops and training to identify racism and develop skills to deal with racism issues. In accordance with the present results, previous studies (Pechenkina et al., 2011; Trudgett, 2009) have demonstrated that the experience of HDR candidates "still remains an isolating experience associated with feelings of exclusion from the mainstream" (p. 16). Several reports (Behrendt et al., 2012; Bradley et al., 2008) have shown that Indigenous Australians, including Indigenous staff and HDR students, experienced racism and a high level of social exclusion. Therefore, Trudgett (2009) suggested that "in order to combat such isolation, social interaction should be encouraged and supported wherever possible" (p. 16). The interest in professional development in identifying and dealing with racism by supervisors of Indigenous HDR students further supports Trudgett's proposal. Overall, supervisors of Indigenous HDR students desired to better prepare themselves to best support their students.

6.5 Summary

This study was designed to investigate the needs and experiences of supervisors of Indigenous HDR students to enable their students to succeed in Australian higher education. This chapter has presented the study's findings about quality supervision from the perspectives of supervisors and revealed the good practices and concerns of supervisors when supervising Indigenous HDR students. In order to better support their students, the importance of professional development for supervisors in cultural awareness, cultural safety and cultural knowledge was highlighted. Also, identifying racism and skills in dealing with racism are critical skills for supervisors. To sum up, our results showed agreement regarding quality supervision from supervisors and Indigenous HDR students' perspectives in the following areas: (1) the understanding and flexible characteristics of supervisors; (2) supervisors' expertise and experience; (3) quality feedback; (4) collaboration with students as a team; (5) building a respectful supervisor–student relationship; (6) supporting Indigenous HDR students personally, physically, mentally and academically.

Notwithstanding the relatively limited sample (33 participants), this work offers valuable insights into understanding the needs and experiences of supervisors of Indigenous HDR students. It is suggested that the study should be repeated with bigger sample size and implemented in a cross-cultural context. An international higher education context would provide a better understanding of the needs and experiences of supervisors internationally. It would also be interesting to have a comparison of how Indigenous HDR students are supported in different countries such as Australia and New Zealand, Canada, the United States and Pacific Oceania countries.

References

Anderson, P., Pham, T., Blue, L., & Fox, A. (2021). Supporting Indigenous higher degree by research students in higher education. In H. Huijser, M. Kek, & F. F. Padró (Eds.), *Student support services* (pp. 1–14). Springer Singapore. https://doi.org/10.1007/978-981-13-3364-4_39-1

Australian Government Department of Education. (2019). *Indigenous students in higher degrees by research. Statistical report, August 2019*. https://www.dese.gov.au/download/4830/indigenous-students-higher-degrees-research/7202/document/pdf

Barney, K. (2016). *Pathways to postgraduate study for Indigenous Australian students: Enhancing the transition to higher degrees by research*. University of Queensland. https://altf.org/wp-content/uploads/2016/08/Barney_NTF_Report_2016.pdf

Behrendt, L., Larkin, S., Griew, R., & Kelly, P. (2012). *Review of higher education access and outcomes for Aboriginal and Torres Strait Islander people* (1922125253). Department of Industry, Innovation, Science, Research and Tertiary Education (Australia).

Bradley, D., Noonan, P., Nugent, H., & Scales, B. (2008). *Review of Australian higher education: Final report* (Bradley review). Department of Education, Employment and Workplace Relations (DEEWR). https://www.voced.edu.au/content/ngv%3A32134

Cardilini, A. P. A., Risely, A., & Richardson, M. F. (2021). Supervising the PhD: Identifying common mismatches in expectations between candidate and supervisor to improve research training outcomes. *Higher Education Research & Development*, 1–15. https://doi.org/10.1080/07294360.2021.1874887

Coopes, R. K. (2007). *Australian Aboriginal marginalisation in policy making and education: A function of colonialism and its aftermath* [Unpublished doctoral thesis]. University of New England.

Durie, M. (2004). Understanding health and illness: Research at the interface between science and Indigenous knowledge. *International Journal of Epidemiology*, 33(5), 1138–1143.

Grant, B., & McKinley, E. (2011). Colouring the pedagogy of doctoral supervision: Considering supervisor, student and knowledge through the lens of indigeneity. *Innovations in Education and Teaching International*, 48(4), 377–386. https://doi.org/10.1080/14703297.2011.617087

Harrison, N., Trudgett, M., & Page, S. (2017). The dissertation examination: Identifying critical factors in the success of Indigenous Australian doctoral students. *Assessment & Evaluation in Higher Education*, 42(1), 115–127. https://doi.org/10.1080/02602938.2015.1085488

Henry, J. (2007). Supervising Aboriginal doctoral candidates. In C. Denholm & T. Evans (Eds.), *Supervising doctorates downunder: Keys to effective supervision in Australia and New Zealand* (pp. 155–163). ACER Press. https://doi.org/10.3316/informit.362200049311181

Hutchings, K., Bainbridge, R., Bodle, K., & Miller, A. (2019). Determinants of attraction, retention and completion for Aboriginal and Torres Strait Islander higher degree research students: A systematic review to inform future research directions. *Research in Higher Education*, 60(2), 245–272. https://doi.org/10.1007/s11162-018-9511-5

Hutchings, K., Bodle, K. A., & Miller, A. (2018). Opportunities and resilience: Enablers to address barriers for Aboriginal and Torres Strait Islander people to commence and complete higher degree research programs. *Australian Aboriginal Studies*, 2, 29–49.

Lariviere, V. (2012). On the shoulders of students? The contribution of PhD students to the advancement of knowledge. *Scientometrics*, 90(2), 463–481. https://doi.org/10.1007/s11192-011-0495-6

Laycock, A., Walker, D., Harrison, N., & Brands, J. (Eds.). (2009). *Supporting Indigenous researchers: A practical guide for supervisors*. The Lowitja Institute.

Moreton-Robinson, A., Anderson, P., Blue, L., Nguyen, L., & Pham, T. (2020). *Report on Indigenous success in higher degree by research*. Australian Government Department of Education and Training. https://eprints.qut.edu.au/199805/

Pechenkina, E., Kowal, E., & Paradies, Y. (2011). Indigenous Australian students' participation rates in higher education: Exploring the role of universities. *The Australian Journal of Indigenous Education*, 40, 59–68. https://doi.org/10.1375/ajie.40.59

Sinclair, J., Barnacle, R., & Cuthbert, D. (2014). How the doctorate contributes to the formation of active researchers: What the research tells us. *Studies in Higher Education (Dorchester-on-Thames), 39*(10), 1972–1986. https://doi.org/10.1080/03075079.2013.806460

Trudgett, M. (2009). Build it and they will come: Building the capacity of Indigenous units in universities to provide better support for Indigenous Australian postgraduate students. *Australian Journal of Indigenous Education, 38*, 9–18.

Trudgett, M. (2011). Western places, academic spaces and Indigenous faces: Supervising Indigenous Australian postgraduate students. *Teaching in Higher Education, 16*(4), 389–399. https://doi.org/10.1080/13562517.2011.560376

Trudgett, M. (2013). Stop, collaborate and listen: A guide to seeding success for Indigenous higher degree research students. In R. Craven & J. Mooney (Eds.), *Seeding success in Indigenous Australian higher education* (Vol. 14, pp. 137–155). Emerald Group Publishing Limited. https://doi.org/10.1108/S1479-3644(2013)0000014006

Trudgett, M. (2014). Supervision provided to Indigenous Australian doctoral students: A black and white issue. *Higher Education Research & Development, 33*(5), 1035–1048. https://doi.org/10.1080/07294360.2014.890576

Universities Australia. (2020). *Indigenous strategy annual report*. https://www.universitiesaustralia.edu.au/wp-content/uploads/2020/02/Indigenous-strategy-second-annual-report.pdf

Wilson, D. (2017). Supervision of Indigenous research students: Considerations for cross-cultural supervisors. *AlterNative: An International Journal of Indigenous Peoples, 13*(4), 256–265. https://doi.org/10.1177/1177180117729771

Open Access This chapter is licensed under the terms of the Creative Commons Attribution 4.0 International License (http://creativecommons.org/licenses/by/4.0/), which permits use, sharing, adaptation, distribution and reproduction in any medium or format, as long as you give appropriate credit to the original author(s) and the source, provide a link to the Creative Commons license and indicate if changes were made.

The images or other third party material in this chapter are included in the chapter's Creative Commons license, unless indicated otherwise in a credit line to the material. If material is not included in the chapter's Creative Commons license and your intended use is not permitted by statutory regulation or exceeds the permitted use, you will need to obtain permission directly from the copyright holder.

Chapter 7
Undoing Commonly Held Beliefs About Indigenous HDR Students

Abstract This chapter draws on our experience facilitating the National Indigenous Research and Knowledges Network (NIRAKN) capacity-building workshops. During these workshops, we continually heard what we refer to as "the three myths about what an Indigenous HDR student ought to be doing". The three myths are that an Indigenous HDR student needs to be: (1) supervised by an Indigenous supervisor; (2) using Indigenous research methodologies; and (3) researching Indigenous issues. Following these workshops, we sought to understand the needs and experience of Indigenous higher degree by research (HDR) students and supervisors of Indigenous HDR students. Informing this chapter are group discussions, written responses and surveys conducted with Indigenous HDR students ($n = 66$) and supervisor of Indigenous HDR students ($n = 33$). In this chapter, we argue against these myths to demonstrate that discipline expertise and/or methodological expertise is the most important variable that determines how all HDR students are paired with supervisors. We also argue that it is harmful and racist to expect Indigenous HDR students to use a prescribed methodology that is race-based. And that, the assumption that Indigenous HDR students should be researching Indigenous matters rather than their own research interests is problematic.

Keywords Indigenous · Higher degree by research · Higher education · Myth · Success · Support

7.1 Introduction

There are many myths surrounding the experiences of Indigenous students in higher education. Indigenous students represent "fewer than one percent of all higher education students" (DEEWR, 2009; as cited in Asmar et al., 2011, p. 1) and have an overall higher attrition and lower completion rates than their non-Indigenous peers (2011). Asmar et al.'s (2011) research, designed to provide an understanding of why Indigenous people in Australia continue to be underrepresented in higher education, revealed many hidden dimensions to Indigenous student engagement and success. For example, it showed that while Indigenous students are less likely to complete their studies, they are "engaged with learning at a similar or slightly higher level than their non-Indigenous peers, and report levels of overall satisfaction equal or higher to their peers" (Asmar et al., 2011, p. 1).

Asmar et al.'s (2011) study, which focused on Indigenous students in higher education, revealed a disparity between interpretation of the statistics and the complex and nuanced reasons why completion rates remain low. They noted that more evidence about factors that contribute to Indigenous students' success is required (Asmar et al., 2011).

It seems that wherever Indigenous students go, the myths follow about what they need in order to complete their research and studies. Through our experience with facilitating capacity-building workshops, interviewing and surveying Indigenous higher degree by research (HDR) students (see Chap. 1 for an overview of the research conducted), we continually heard what we refer to as "the three myths about what an Indigenous HDR student should be doing" throughout their studies. These myths are that an Indigenous HDR student should be:

- Supervised by an Indigenous supervisor
- Using Indigenous research methodologies
- Researching Indigenous issues.

Indigenous HDR enrolments have "increased over the last decade but completion rates remain relatively low" (Moreton-Robinson et al., 2020, p. 3). There are a number of factors contributing to these low completion rates (Moreton-Robinson et al., 2020), and in this chapter, we argue that the needs of Indigenous HDR students are being consistently misunderstood, which may lead to lower rates of satisfaction with their studies, along with these low completion rates. This chapter interrogates the three myths to break down the problems with each of these assumptions. It provides an overview of what Indigenous HDR students have told us they need in order to complete their studies.

7.2 Data Used to Inform This Chapter

The group discussion and individual written responses were obtained in 2018 following a National Indigenous Research and Knowledges Network (NIRAKN) capacity-building workshop for Indigenous HDRs across Australia. Three separate group discussions took place; however, it was impossible to identify the participants from one another, so this data was labelled 'GD_IndigenousHDR'. The written responses were completed individually, and therefore, we can identify each participant by number. The group discussions were audio recorded and transcribed. The transcribed group discussions were then uploaded into NVivo with the individual written responses. Both datasets were read in NVivo where the text was highlighted and coded to identify emerging themes. The online surveys that were completed by

Indigenous HDR students and supervisors of Indigenous HDR students were developed using the Qualtrics online platform. The responses from both surveys were uploaded in NVivo so that they could be read, tagged and coded into themes. In total four datasets were used to inform this chapter (Table 7.1).

7.3 Myth One: Indigenous HDR Students Need to Be Supervised by Indigenous Supervisor

> It's got nothing to do with culture and that stuff, I just need to know that I'm safe and supported (GD_IndigenousHDR).

The first myth about Indigenous HDR students is that the students must have Indigenous supervisors. This myth seems to have stemmed from the limited research in the area, which has until now focused "on the impact of cultural aspects on the student–supervisor relationship" (Moreton-Robinson et al., 2020, p. 8). Previous studies have reported the importance of culturally appropriate supervision for Indigenous students without the data to demonstrate how this "culturally appropriate supervision enables" them to succeed, (Moreton-Robinson et al., 2020, p. 11). With just 431 Indigenous academics employed in Australian universities in 2018 (Department of Education and Training, 2020, as cited in Moreton-Robinson et al., 2020), there are simply not enough to supervise the number of Indigenous students currently enrolled in HDR studies (Hutchings et al., 2018; Trudgett, 2011). With this knowledge, the research has shifted to make recommendations for non-Indigenous supervisors, such as requiring them to undertake cultural awareness training and involve non-academic community members in the supervisory team, and a database of academics who are in a position to supervise Indigenous students (Trudgett, 2011). These findings are focused on the impact of cultural aspects on the student–supervisor relationships, supervisors' mentoring expertise and their availability and respect, as well as age and gender being contributing factors to the quality of Indigenous HDR supervision (Moreton-Robinson et al., 2020).

Although prior research places an emphasis on culturally appropriate supervision, "there is no importance attributed to disciplinary knowledge in the production of new knowledge" which is "a criterion to be met in the examination of the dissertation" (Moreton-Robinson et al., 2020, p. 12) as well as the value of this that our research has shown to be an important variable perceived by Indigenous students as an indicator of quality HDR supervision. While our research demonstrates some disparity between students' expectations (wants) and their actual needs and how they are met by the supervisors, which results in a disconnection between the students' understanding of the supervisory process' and the 'institutional requirements of supervision' (see Chap. 1), what was clear in our data is the value of supervisors' disciplinary knowledge. When asked their perception of quality supervision, one Indigenous HDR student said: "Excellence in discipline, great communicator, high level

Table 7.1 Datasets used to inform this chapter

Dataset number	Type (written evaluation form, group discussion, written response and/or online survey)	Year collected	What it is and who it includes	Number of participants	Referred to in text as
3	Group discussion (qualitative)	2018	Discussion about needs and experiences of Indigenous HDRs (Indigenous HDR students)	34	GD_IndigenousHDR
4	Individual written responses (qualitative)	2018	Written responses about needs and experiences of Indigenous HDR students (Indigenous HDR students)	34[a]	IWR_IndigenousHDR#
5	Online survey (qualitative and quantitative demographic information)	2020	Survey about the needs and experiences of Indigenous HDR students (Indigenous HDR students)	32	OLS2_IndigenousHDR#
6	Online survey (qualitative and quantitative demographic information)	2020	Survey about the needs and experiences of Indigenous HDR students (supervisors and Indigenous HDR students)	33	OLS3_Supervisor#
Total participants				99	

[a]The same participants who completed the group discussion also provided a written response to additional questions. We only counted these participants once despite it being two different sets of data

understanding of the policy and processes, high level of support/guidance of navigating the 'academy'" (IWR_IndigenousHDR20). This response places emphasis on the supervisor's discipline knowledge as well as their understanding of the institutional demands of their university and the academy as a whole, which supports our concern that previous research has paid little attention to how supervisors support their students to completion by ensuring they meet the institutional requirements of the degree (Moreton-Robinson et al., 2020).

To the same question, another student answered:

> A supervisor slash [sic] supervisors who are experienced in your field and who can support you through each milestone in a way that complements your working style … [and] sensitivity—not specifically culturally—but to the needs of your project/goals. A strong comment driven personality (IWR_IndigenousHDR29).

Although we agree with many of the recommendations made in previous research by Laycock et al. (2009), Schofield et al. (2013), and Trudgett (2011, 2014), our research demonstrates that more emphasis should be placed on the importance of disciplinary and institutional knowledge when matching students with supervisors. While feelings of cultural safety should not be overlooked as important factors contributing to Indigenous HDR student success, it is possible for Indigenous students to successfully complete their research with the support of non-Indigenous supervisors.

All three of the Indigenous authors of this book chose non-Indigenous supervisors based on their discipline expertise. For instance, Melanie Saward chose the primary supervisor for her Master of Fine Arts (Research) based on their discipline knowledge and understanding of the specific subject she was researching, and her associate supervisor was assigned by the university. Neither of her supervisors were Indigenous, and during her research, she felt that both supported her through her milestones in a way that set her up for success—so much so that she chose to continue the relationship for her PhD. At the Queensland University of Technology, Indigenous HDR students are provided with additional support via the Carumba Institute, and in many cases—certainly in Melanie's experience—the support provided by Indigenous academics and staff can take up the responsibility for providing some cultural support for students when navigating the academic space. This is, of course, one case of one Indigenous student who had a positive experience with non-Indigenous supervisors; not all Indigenous students will have the same unique set of needs and expectations, and not every university is equipped with the facilities to support the specific requirements of Indigenous HDR students. Some of our HDR student participants noted that some of the downfalls to having non-Indigenous supervisors were a lack of knowledge of 'Indigenous stuff' (GD_IndigenousHDR); lack of familiarity with the high-level ethics process required when undertaking research involving Indigenous people (GD_IndigenousHDR); "not having a strong understanding of Indigenous perspectives, theories, [and] methodologies" (IWR_IndigenousHDR20); and "a need for supervisors to understand all the different directions that Indigenous students are often pulled in" (GD_IndigenousHDR).

The assumption that Indigenous HDR students must have Indigenous supervisors also creates a demand that universities struggle to meet. With so few Indigenous people completing HDR studies, often institutions will offer promotions to graduates very early in their careers. One student noted that they had sought out a particular supervisor "because I was told if you're an Aboriginal you need an Aboriginal supervisor and this was who was available to me" (GD_IndigenousHDR). The student says that this supervisor had been "offered a professorship almost straight after finishing [their] PhD ... [they have] never supervised a student to completion" (GD_IndigenousHDR). The student said that this was obviously having an effect on their supervisor's work and had a 'flow-on effect' to the students as well (GD_IndigenousHDR). The student said "I don't need that cultural support. I've got that from my family and from my elders. What I really needed was a good supervisor" (GD_IndigenousHDR).

A concerning comment about the lack of support from an Indigenous supervisor may be explained by a poor practice that some universities adopt by allocating Indigenous supervisors to Indigenous HDR students despite them not having the discipline knowledge. A participant in a group discussion said: "I have an Indigenous supervisor as my second. That supervisor does nothing, never offers feedback, doesn't come to meetings" (GD_IndigenousHDR).

However, there appears to be a misbelief circling in universities that Indigenous HDR students should be placed with Indigenous academies. Out findings do not support placing Indigenous HDR students with supervisors who do not have disciplinary knowledge regardless of whether the academic is Indigenous or non-Indigenous. A recurrent theme in the group discussions and individual written responses was a sense among interviewees that supervisors' unavailability was a big concern for their research journey. As one interviewee put it:

> She [supervisor] is always too busy to read my work. She didn't forward the paperwork that means I had to wait for 4 months for second supervisors. I discussed this with graduate school. My supervisor and the school blamed each other. No one followed up my questions (GD_IndigenousHDR).

We also found from the capacity-building workshops for Indigenous HDR students that it is important to remind students that they have agency and can change supervisors if the relationship is not working.

Another Indigenous HDR student revealed that their supervisor does not reply to messages, is never available and does not follow up on work they have offered. The students also discussed the power difference in relationships which may mean students do not feel comfortable to follow up requests with their supervisors.

We want to see the number of Indigenous academics increase so that any student who wants to have an Indigenous supervisor has that choice, but—perhaps ironically—in order for this to become reality, the belief that Indigenous HDR students must have Indigenous supervisors must change. If the myth that Indigenous students cannot be appropriately supervised to completion without having an Indigenous supervisor does not stop, we cannot expect retention and completion rates to improve. In order to improve outcomes for Indigenous HDR students, more attention should be placed on students being matched with supervisors with appropriate disciplinary background, institutional knowledge and cultural appreciation of Indigenous perspectives. One Indigenous HDR student captured this sentiment by stating that they believe that a good supervisor would have "cultural understanding support from an Indigenous perspective and the capacity to evaluate Indigenous understandings that are supportive of these concepts" (OLS2_IndigenousHDR2).

7.4 Myth Two: Indigenous HDR Students Need to Use Indigenous Research Methodologies

> Statistical experimental design and advanced literature searches are also quite useful (OLS2_IndigenousHDR5).

The second myth is that Indigenous HDR students need to use Indigenous research methodologies. This myth often goes hand in hand with the expectation that Indigenous HDR students must have Indigenous supervisors. The assumption here is that non-Indigenous supervisors do not have a pre-existing understanding of Indigenous research methodologies and therefore will not be able to provide appropriate support. There are several issues with this assumption. First, Indigenous research methodologies do not exist solely for the use of Indigenous students and academics, and they are available for all to use. Second, it is racist to expect that Indigenous HDR students use a prescribed methodology that is race based.

7.4.1 Indigenous Research Methodologies

> Yeah, don't tokenise us. Why are we seen as so different from every HDR student (GD_IndigenousHDR)?

Indigenous research methodologies are available for the use of all scholars and researchers, not just those who identify as Indigenous. Our experience has shown that when non-Indigenous supervisors express discomfort in supervising Indigenous students, one of the assumptions they are making is that these students will need or want to use Indigenous research methodologies and, as a participant in our supervisor survey (who identified as being neither Aboriginal or Torres Strait Islander) noted: "I am always worried that I am out of my depth, especially in relation to the theoretical" (OLS3_Supervisor6).

Indigenous research methodologies are available for everyone to read, study, gain an understanding of and use. In fact, we argue that in order to increase the number of Indigenous academics and remove the unnecessary burdens from those few Indigenous people currently working in the academy, it is critical that all academics engage with Indigenous methodologies. This is regardless of whether they are currently supervising Indigenous students and/or whether the students they are supervising are using Indigenous research methodologies.

With reviews of higher education and research training systems in Australia highlighting the need to increase Indigenous HDR students' participation (Behrendt et al., 2012; McGagh et al., 2016) as a way of transforming "the Indigenous professional class" and reshaping "the research practices of tertiary institutions" (Moreton-Robinson et al., 2020, p. 6), it is critical that non-Indigenous academics researchers and academics "self-interrogate [their] contributions to, and alignments with, ongoing colonizing practices by way of conducting research … *on* (as opposed to *with*) Indigenous peoples" (Blair, 2016; Moreton-Robinson, 2000, 2006; Nakata, 2007, as cited in Krusz et al., 2020, p. 206).

Although there is a demonstrated understanding from supervisors that they need more professional development to better support Indigenous HDR students, when participants in our supervisor online survey were asked if they thought supervisors of Indigenous HDR students required professional development, 5 out of 33 respondents specifically mentioned the need for supervisors to understand Indigenous research methodologies (OLS3_Supervisor7, 25, 27, 28, 29). Many emphasised a need for cultural awareness training. While we agree that cultural awareness training can be helpful and institutions should be offering this training to all staff members, we see these responses as a lack of understanding of areas that would be of specific benefit to Indigenous HDR students, not to mention having a broader effect on decolonising across their own research, teaching and practices. It is important, too, to remember that cultural awareness training is broad and may not be applicable to individual HDR students who are not, as we have mentioned before, a monolith and come from many different communities and countries and have different levels of cultural engagement.

One participant also noted that they "felt supervisors of Indigenous HDR students should have training that is led 'by Indigenous staff'" (OLS3_Supervisor33) and another said that supervisors should "meet with other Indigenous scholars and students – to talk about Indigenous research methodologies" (OLS3_Supervisor22). In many institutions, the work of building Indigenous HDR student capacity and doing the work of decolonising falls to Indigenous academics. As already noted in this chapter, there are very few Indigenous academics employed by Australian institutions, so when non-Indigenous academics expect Indigenous academics to take on additional work of providing cultural awareness training, they are further adding to the burden and labour of their colleagues. When it comes to supervising HDR students, this again goes hand in hand with the assumption that Indigenous HDRs should have a co-supervisor who is Indigenous. We feel this demonstrates that these supervisors believe it is the Indigenous academic's role to provide cultural and Indigenous methodological support while it is their role to provide discipline-specific support. However, there is no reason they cannot engage with, and understand and use Indigenous research methodologies and support any student who wishes to use them, regardless of whether the student is Indigenous.

Although we would like to see Indigenous methodologies form a key part of mandatory professional development for supervisors of Indigenous HDR students, as noted by respondents above, the idea that academics should wait to be trained in these areas is problematic. The research and literature needed to start engaging with Indigenous methodologies are already available to these supervisors, and we would like to see them stepping up and taking the initiative to learn. To apply Moreton-Robinson's (2000) work on decolonising feminism to the academic space, she said that decolonising "requires more than including voice or making space for Indigenous [people]" (p. 351). To do this, non-Indigenous people must initiate "and engage in dialogue with each other, rather than inappropriately requesting or expecting direction … from Indigenous colleagues" (Krusz et al., 2020, p. 206). This can also be applied to non-Indigenous academics who already have the tools available to them in order to take the initiative and interest in Indigenous research methodologies without being prompted by the supervision of Indigenous HDR students or by their Indigenous colleagues.

7.4.2 Indigenous Research Methodologies: Use Is Not Compulsory

> I expect my Indigenous students to complete a project that makes a contribution to their community (OLS3_Supervisor12).

Although we argue that all researchers and academics should develop an understanding of Indigenous research methodologies, we also argue the assumption that every Indigenous student will want—or need—to use Indigenous research methodologies demonstrates a problematic homogenisation and othering of Indigenous people. It also shows a concerning lack of focus on the institutional requirements of HDR studies.

At our home institution, the Queensland University of Technology (QUT), the guidelines for examiners of PhD theses state that a thesis is expected to show evidence of: originality of the research data and/or analysis of the data; coherence of argument and presentation; competence in technical and conceptual analysis; and contextual competence (QUT, n.d.). It does not, however, state that Indigenous students must use Indigenous research methodologies, just as it does not state that non-Indigenous students must use a methodology specific to their race, culture or other identity. Yet, during our time facilitating workshops for the National Indigenous Research and Knowledges Network (NIRAKN), many students, including one of the authors of this book, Melanie Saward, were asked which Indigenous research methodologies they were including in their research. Another of this book's author, Levon Blue, was told by one of her supervisors that she should use talking circles when conducting research in the First Nation community during her PhD. The advice was not followed; instead, Levon was led by the Community members she interviewed, which was one on one and group interviews that were audio recorded.

Indigenous HDR students are negotiators of complex intersections (Nakata et al., 2015, p. 140) between their own experiences and standpoints as Indigenous people, their research and the institutional requirements of their degrees. They work in contested spaces (Nakata et al., 2015) with Western education systems having their roots in colonialism and being "based on a foundation of oppressive ideologies of assimilation" aligning to the dispossession of Indigenous people (Pihama et al., 2019, p. 52). For this reason, we believe it is important that Indigenous HDR students are given the opportunity to engage with Indigenous research methodologies—if they choose to—regardless of whether they are including them in their research or not. But, as the engineers and controllers of their research, it is up to the student to choose the most appropriate methodological framework for their research and discipline. Though Indigenous HDR students work in these contested spaces, Western knowledge systems are an important site for Indigenous intellectual and critical inquiry, for it is from this location, that Indigenous students articulate their own position, "forged … from within their own experiences of being Indigenous" (Nakata et al., 2015, p. 142).

This means that for some Indigenous HDR students, using Indigenous research methodologies may not be the most appropriate fit for their research. A participant in our online supervisor survey specifically noted a need for supervisors of Indigenous HDRs to have training that would help supervisors to "better understand the ramifications of the imposition of Western education systems and how this plays out at the HDR level" (OLS3_Supervisor4). We are not arguing that the imposition of Western education systems has not had and will not have an effect on Indigenous HDR students, but our data demonstrated that when responding to their perception of supervising Indigenous HDR students, very few had considered that their students might not want or need to use Indigenous research methodologies.

In research on employment, Indigenous people are constantly negotiating "between different systems of thinking and practice, and understanding of people's historical experience of these intersections" (Nakata et al., 2015, p. 142). The Australian Government's Review of Higher Education Access and Outcomes for Aboriginal and Torres Strait Islander People Final Report by Behrendt et al. (2012) suggests that universities offer participation activities such as "capacity building, mentoring, peer support, tutoring" and so on to "better meet the needs of students" (p. 26). Through our experience of running capacity-building research, we have interacted with many students who have noted that this separate mode of delivery has provided them with a good grounding in Indigenous research methodologies. For one of the authors of this book, Melanie Saward, participating in Indigenous research methodologies masterclasses and workshops as an HDR student helped her to negotiate the intersections between Western knowledge systems and discipline-specific skills, despite the fact that her master's research did not use any Indigenous research methodologies. She used knowledge gained at this training to negotiate a space between the academic process and her identity as an Indigenous person. Many students who participated in our workshops and training had similar experiences, and although we do not expect that students who participate will necessarily apply their learnings to their research, we understand that we are providing Indigenous students with "strategies for working within the disciplines to uphold Indigenous standpoints" (Nakata et al., 2015, p. 142). Nakata et al. (2015) described an approach that:

is likely to have bearing on the quality of Indigenous students' preparation for professional practice in a range of Indigenous contexts; for example, in health practice, governance areas, economic development, law, and business. Working in these contexts requires constant negotiation between different systems of thinking and practice, and understanding of people's historical experience of these intersections. Indigenous learners' engagement with the disciplines is a specific, specialised example of what Indigenous Australians deal with every day as they interact with broader institutional practices and conventions (p. 142).

Indigenous research methodologies are important tools for research and are available for everyone—Indigenous or not—to read, understand and apply to their research and practice. We want to see more academics actively and autonomously engaging with these methodologies as we believe it will make them better supervisors and allies. But while we want to see supervisors finding a new understanding of Indigenous research methodologies, it is important that they do not impose race-based methodologies on the Indigenous HDR students they are supervising if they are not the most appropriate methodologies for the student's research. As an Indigenous HDR student noted "although I'm not doing cultural studies, it is still important [my supervisors] understand that Indigenous issues/practices/relatedness/history/family [are] all important" (IWR_IndigenousHDR30).

7.5 Myth Three: Indigenous HDR Students Should Be Researching Indigenous Issues

> Don't assume that because I'm Aboriginal I want to discuss every racist event that comes up in the media, introduce me to the practices and people that helped you succeed (OLS2_IndigenousHDR19).

The assumption that Indigenous HDR students should be researching Indigenous matters rather than their own research interests is problematic. Many Indigenous HDR students have shared with us that they were told that their theses were not Indigenous enough and had been given recommendations to incorporate more Indigeneity into their theses. A non-Indigenous supervisor who participated in our online survey noted that they expect their Indigenous students to "complete a project that makes a contribution to their community" (OLS3_Supervisor12). There are problematic aspects to this assumption, with one important one being: are non-Indigenous students expected to complete a project that makes a contribution to their communities? Or are they simply expected to meet the institutional requirements of their research?

Like their non-Indigenous colleagues, Indigenous HDR students undertake research for myriad reasons. While some will wish to make contributions to their communities, others are exploring art and practice, upskilling for employment or researching as a part of a team. Just as it may not be appropriate in some contexts for students to introduce Indigenous methodologies into their research, some students will have research interests that do not relate to Indigeneity and it is problematic for supervisors to assume that they will need to do so.

7.6 Summary

Undoing commonly held beliefs about the needs and wants of Indigenous HDR students is critical if we are to see better retention and completion rates and in order to see our aim of a robust Indigenous academic workforce come to fruition. To do this, we suggest that supervisors of Indigenous HDR students engage in critical reading, research and discussion of Indigenous research methodologies, being careful to not expect their Indigenous colleagues to do the work of delivering training or facilitating these discussions. Non-Indigenous supervisors need to understand the challenges facing Indigenous HDR students and academics and work with their colleagues to better support their students, understanding that it may not always be possible for Indigenous HDRs to have Indigenous supervisors, that they may not need or wish to use Indigenous research methodologies in their research and they may choose not to research Indigenous issues.

References

Asmar, C., Page, S., & Radloff, A. (2011). *Dispelling myths: Indigenous students' engagement with university*. AUSSE Research Briefings, v.10.

Behrendt, L., Larkin, S., Griew, R., & Kelly, P. (2012). *Review of higher education access and outcomes for Aboriginal and Torres Strait Islander people* (1922125253). Department of Industry, Innovation, Science, Research and Tertiary Education (Australia).

Blair, N. (2016). Researched to death: Indigenous peoples talking up our experiences of research. *International Review of Qualitative Research, 8*, 463–478.

Hutchings, K., Bodle, K. A., & Miller, A. (2018). Opportunities and resilience: Enablers to address barriers for Aboriginal and Torres Strait Islander people to commence and complete higher degree research programs. *Australian Aboriginal Studies, 2*, 29–49.

Krusz, E., Davey, T., Wigginton, B., & Hall, N. (2020). What contributions, if any, can non-Indigenous researchers offer toward decolonizing health research? *Qualitative Health Research, 30*(2), 205–216. https://doi.org/10.1177/1049732319861

Laycock, A., Walker, D., Harrison, N., & Brands, J. (2009). *Supporting Indigenous researchers: A practical guide for supervisors*. The Lowitja Institute.

McGagh, J., Marsh, H., Western, M., Thomas, P., Hastings, A., Mihailova, M., & Wenham, M. (2016). *Review of Australia's research training system*. https://acola.org/wp-content/uploads/2018/08/saf13-review-research-training-system-report.pdf

Moreton-Robinson, A. (2000). *Talkin' up to the white woman*. University of Queensland Press.

Moreton-Robinson, A. (2006). Whiteness matters: Implications of talkin' up to the white woman. *Australian Feminist Studies, 21*(50), 245–256.

Moreton-Robinson, A., Anderson, P., Blue, L., Nguyen, L., & Pham, T. (2020). *Report on Indigenous success in higher degrees by research*. https://eprints.qut.edu.au/199805/1/49092585.pdf

Nakata, M., Nakata, V., & Chin, M. (2015). Approaches to the academic preparation and support of Indigenous students for tertiary studies. *The Australian Journal of Indigenous Education, 37*(S1), 137–145. https://doi.org/10.1375/S1326011100000478

Pihama, L., Lee-Morgan, J., Tuhiwai Smith, L., Tiakiwai, S. J., & Seed-Pihama, J. (2019). MAI Te Kupenga: Supporting Māori and Indigenous doctoral scholars within higher education. *AlterNative: An International Journal of Indigenous Peoples, 15*(1), 52–61. https://doi.org/10.1177/1177180119828065

References

Queensland University of Technology (QUT). (n.d.). *Examination of doctor of philosophy thesis notes for the guidance of examiners.* https://qutvirtual4.qut.edu.au/group/staff/research/higher-degree-research/thesis-editing-and-examination/thesis-examination

Schofield, T., O'Brien, R., & Gilroy, J. (2013). Indigenous higher education: Overcoming barriers to participation in research higher degree programs. *Australian Aborginal Studies, 13,* 13–28.

Trudgett, M. (2011). Western places, academic spaces and Indigenous faces: Supervising Indigenous Australian postgraduate students. *Training in Higher Education, 16*(4), 1035–1048.

Trudgett, M. (2014). Supervision provided to Indigenous Australian doctoral students: A black and white issue. *Higher Education Research & Development, 35*(5), 1035–1048.

Open Access This chapter is licensed under the terms of the Creative Commons Attribution 4.0 International License (http://creativecommons.org/licenses/by/4.0/), which permits use, sharing, adaptation, distribution and reproduction in any medium or format, as long as you give appropriate credit to the original author(s) and the source, provide a link to the Creative Commons license and indicate if changes were made.

The images or other third party material in this chapter are included in the chapter's Creative Commons license, unless indicated otherwise in a credit line to the material. If material is not included in the chapter's Creative Commons license and your intended use is not permitted by statutory regulation or exceeds the permitted use, you will need to obtain permission directly from the copyright holder.

Chapter 8
What We Need for Success: Recommendations and Wishes

Abstract Throughout this book, we have shared our experiences of conducting capacity-building workshops and undertaking research about the needs and experiences of Indigenous HDR students in Australia. In total, we heard from 147 participants which included 113 Indigenous HDR students across Australia and 34 supervisors of Indigenous HDR students. The insights received from both Indigenous HDR students and supervisors revealed that there are still opportunities to improve the HDR experience for Indigenous students. Based on our findings, in this chapter, we expand on the recommendations outlined in the Moreton-Robinson et al.'s (Report on Indigenous success in higher degree by research. Prepared for the Australian Government, Department of Education and Training, 2020) report to include new data collected in 2020 from 32 Indigenous HDR students. We hope our recommendations, once acted upon, will have a positive impact on the success of Indigenous HDR students and that the insights shared by the Indigenous HDR candidates we heard from will have meaning and relevance for anyone pursuing a research degree.

Keywords Indigenous HDR students · Higher degree by research · Recommendations · Higher education · Success

8.1 Overview

The recommendations we outline in this chapter are based on the newly collected data from 32 Indigenous HDR students from across Australia. Although the recommendations are about ways to improve the success of Indigenous HDRs in Australia, we believe our findings may also be of relevance to other countries with Indigenous populations, including New Zealand, Canada, the United States and Mexico. For example, in New Zealand, there is concern about the under-representation of Māori students in higher education and reports of students encountering obstacles to access higher education (Barnhardt, 2002; McKinley et al., 2011; Schofield et al., 2013; Wilson et al., 2011). Māori students were also reported to experience cultural effacement and alienation similar to Indigenous Australians' experiences of university education (Barnhardt, 2002; Wilson et al., 2011). Cultural effacement and alienation are factors reported to be discouraging Indigenous students from participating in higher education in Canada (Hauser et al., 2009), Mexico (Schmelkes, 2009) and Australia (Schofield et al., 2013), although universities in New Zealand, Canada and Mexico have responded to these issues with a range of approaches.

We are attempting to provide evidence-informed recommendations that may further support for Indigenous HDR students to complete their research degree. Despite our focus on Australia, we believe the findings reported in this book will be of value to Indigenous HDR students, supervisors of Indigenous HDR students, policy-makers at institutions and national leaders globally who are advocating for better conditions for Indigenous HDR students. The insights received from both Indigenous HDR students and supervisors of Indigenous HDR students in this book reveal that there are still opportunities to improve the HDR experience for Indigenous HDR students.

In this chapter, we expand on the recommendations outlined in the Moreton-Robinson et al.'s (2020) report, which included recommendations to: (1) advise Indigenous HDR students on the role of supervisors and the boundaries of that role; (2) instruct supervisors of Indigenous HDR students to be accountable for students' academic success, schedule regular meetings and provide high quality feedback; (3) advocate that higher education institutions ensure that students are supervised by a team of academics who possess relevant disciplinary knowledge and mentoring experience and who value Indigenous knowledges and cultures; and (4) urge national education policy makers to establish a national framework to support collaboration between Indigenous and non-Indigenous academics.

8.2 Data Used to Inform This Chapter

Moreton-Robinson et al. (2020) report was informed by the group discussions and individual written responses that took place in 2018 (see Chap. 1 for the complete list of datasets). This chapter has been informed by data collected from 32 Indigenous HDR students who completed an online survey in 2020 (see Table 8.1). The completed surveys were downloaded and saved in an Excel spreadsheet and then uploaded into NVivo for analysis purposes. We read the responses and highlighted sections to code the responses and identify themes. Informing this chapter are specific questions we asked Indigenous HDR students about what they wished they could tell their supervisor to improve the relationship and what Indigenous HDR students would tell prospective HDR candidates.

We have incorporated the new data obtained from dataset 5 to make the following additional recommendations as part of quality supervision practices. These include: (1) offering career development advice to Indigenous HDR students seeking an academic career; (2) mentoring Indigenous HDR students throughout their candidature; and (3) providing ongoing research training initiatives for Indigenous HDR students. Although the additional recommendations can be incorporated into supervision practices, they may also need to be supported from within academia. For

Table 8.1 Dataset used to inform this chapter

Dataset number	Type (written evaluation form, group discussion, written response and/or online survey)	Year collected	What it is and who it includes	Number of participants	Referred to in text as
5	Online survey (qualitative and quantitative demographic information)	2020	Survey about the needs and experiences of Indigenous HDR students (Indigenous HDR students)	32	OLS2_IndigenousHDR#
Total participants				32	

instance, we know that Indigenous academics are under-represented in higher education institutions across Australia (Moreton-Robinson et al., 2020). Therefore, greater efforts to encourage Indigenous HDR students into academic careers should be fostered during their research degrees. Having institutional support and targets could help to ensure this opportunity to increase Indigenous HDR pathways into academia is met. Similarly, ensuring that ongoing research training opportunities are available to Indigenous HDR students may also require a budget and approval from the school and/or faculty the student is enrolled in.

8.3 Recommendations for Higher Education Institutions

One way that universities can help to increase the number of Indigenous academics employed is to establish pathways for Indigenous HDRs students to obtain academic roles during their candidature. For instance, co-author Melanie Saward is completing her PhD at the Queensland University of Technology (QUT) and was offered a pre-to-post doctoral appointment. This three-year Level A academic appointment means that Melanie is on a full-time salary, and completing a PhD is part of the research component making up 70% of her duties. The teaching duties make up 20% and are based on Melanie's discipline expertise in creative writing. The remaining 10% is service and involves peer-reviewing journal articles and/or participating in committees. Following the successful completion of the PhD, a Level B position in the school will be offered to Melanie. This arrangement is only possible because the university agreed to increase the number of Indigenous academics and approved this scheme.

8.4 Recommendations for Supervisors

Faculty allocation of supervisors to Indigenous HDR students should be based on supervisors with the necessary discipline knowledge and/or methodological expertise required. Where possible, we encourage Indigenous HDR students to seek out the supervisors they are hoping to work with based on the discipline and/or methodological expertise. The importance of accepting the role of supervisor comes with a commitment to the student and interest in their proposed project. Noting that workload issues can have an impact on supervisors' availability, but that time is needed to ensure that they can meet with their students, provide constructive feedback and support Indigenous HDR students to be successful in their research journey.

Trudgett's (2011) framework of best practice for supervision includes four categories, including academic skills-based support from supervisors, personal reflection of supervisor, responsibilities of university and responsibilities of national bodies. The findings of this current study added more suggestions from Indigenous HDR students for supervisors, including that: (1) supervisors should set clear expectations for HDR students from the beginning of their research study; (2) supervisors should support HDR students and mentor students to develop a research career; (3) HDR students should be supervised by qualified supervisors with the discipline knowledge the student is seeking; and (4) supervisors need to make time to support their students.

Together, these findings provide important insights into the perspectives and experiences of Indigenous HDR students in research supervision. We also asked Indigenous HDR students' what suggestions they had to improve supervision practices. Students reported that to improve the quality of supervision, the relationships between Indigenous HDR students and their supervisors needed to be both effective and comfortable. The remaining recommendations come from Indigenous HDR students.

8.5 Students' Suggestions for Improved Supervision

An Indigenous HDR student suggested:

> For my non-Indigenous supervisor, before supervising an Indigenous student, take an Indigenous studies unit at uni as a student and learn. Be open to challenging your assumptions. Sit in the position of learner rather than expert and understand that your student has the right to tackle this thesis in the way that they want to (OLS2_IndigenousHDR1).

Another Indigenous HDR student echoed the message above by highlighting the systemic racism that persists and how understanding is needed to ensure Indigenous HDR students succeed in higher education institutions.

> Academia is a scary place for many of us, and institutions have been incredibly unkind to First Nations people historically, and we still live in a world where racism is extremely prevalent and where white supremacy is very much alive and can at times dictate the courses of our

8.5 Students' Suggestions for Improved Supervision

lives. There are systemic implications for challenging those hegemonic structures, and there are lifelong consequences which present themselves in the form of trauma responses and ongoing triggers that limit our participation and well-being in those spaces. There are reasons for disengagement, reticence, and aversion that sometimes non-Indigenous supervisors will fail to comprehend. This is why cultural reflexivity, cultural responsiveness and social and intellectual flexibilities are important. It is potentially the difference between who succeeds and who fails in Indigenous HDR (OLS2_IndigenousHDR4).

In the interest of fostering success for Indigenous HDR students, one asked that supervisors remain positive and hold high expectations of this student:

> Be accessible! Show an interest! Give positive feedback first, then constructive feedback! Support HDR students so they can develop a belief in themselves that they are capable. Build them up emotionally and educationally so they can stick with it for the long haul. Don't give up on HDR students or they will give up on themselves (OLS2_IndigenousHDR6).

On the other hand, Indigenous HDR students do not want their supervisors to think that they already know everything needed to complete a research degree:

> Teach your students the processes of academy and the institution. I have had previous supervisors that either did not know or would not tell me things like how the methodology chapter works. I now have supervisors who are very prescriptive about the methodology chapter structure and it's super helpful (OLS2_IndigenousHDR9).

Another student shared similar thoughts but also pointed out that they wished to stay focused on completing the research degree and learning how their supervisors succeeded:

> Don't assume I know things even though I appear very capable (this is pretty tricky, I realise). Don't assume that because I'm Aboriginal I want to discuss every racist event that comes up in the media, introduce me to the practices and people that helped you succeed (OLS2_IndigenousHDR19).

The additional responsibilities that some Indigenous HDR students face involve Community obligations that arise at various times including during the death of a Community member:

> Understand that for me, community obligations, deaths, responsibilities, are different than your non-Indigenous students and all these things impact. I am sorry for that but there is little I can do (OLS2_IndigenousHDR31).

The need for understanding and extension on milestones might be needed to ensure Indigenous HDR students can complete both requirements to their studies and their community. Another Indigenous HDR student pointed out how their research degree is something that also has to stand up outside academia and needs to be something they feel proud of:

> Guide us and make suggestions – but understand that this is our journey and we are governed by ourselves and our culture in what we produce and we have to be able to stand proudly by the finished work (OLS2_IndigenousHDR28).

Another student highlighted the importance of meeting the students about where they are regarding feedback. Being flexible about the condition of the writing may lead to more opportunities for the Indigenous HDR student to learn from their supervisors about what the thesis needs to look like:

> More time to provide feedback and have a conversation. Flexibility in feedback, that is, working with students' feedback needs rather than setting the standard that all reviewed writing must be in final draft mode (OLS2_IndigenousHDR13).

The importance of engaging with the students work and correspondence was noted by one student that "make a point of reading applications and emails carefully. It is obvious to the student when either hasn't been read" (OLS2_IndigenousHDR8).

Many Indigenous HDR students also reported that they were happy with their supervisors and that they did not need to change anything. The need to spark interest, motivate, guide and expose Indigenous HDR students to the opportunities that lie within the academy was also reported. In the next section, we share the recommendations that Indigenous HDR students had for prospective HDR students.

8.6 Recommendations for Prospective Indigenous HDR Students

When we asked Indigenous HDR students what recommendations they would provide to someone thinking about enrolling in a research degree, they had plenty of advice to share. One Indigenous HDR student recommended that they "love your subject area – if you aren't driven and passionate it will be hard slog!" The need to be driven by passion was also shared by another HDR student who suggested that students:

> Study something you are passionate about, otherwise I don't think you will enjoy it. Also, if possible, try to study full time by obtaining a scholarship or something similar so you don't have to worry about an income or studying and working at the same time, otherwise it can get too much and your study can be put off (OLS2_IndigenousHDR34).

The important of understanding why you are pursuing a research degree was also mentioned. This participant suggested questioning your motivation: "Is it for your career? Is it for pleasure/interest? These are two very different motivations" (OLS2_IndigenousHDR16). If it is career related, a different approach to candidature might be taken as the need to build a competitive CV along the way is often recommended. Another Indigenous HDR student summarised three key factors in a successful HDR journey:

> The three most important factors for considering a HDR are (1) whether or not you have access to adequate financial support, (2) finding a supervisor with whom you can have a positive and productive relationship, and (3) ensuring that you have good social and emotional well-being support (OLS2_IndigenousHDR25).

The need for support was also shared by another participant who recommended "finding an Indigenous cohort or HDR community as it's lonely" (OLS2_IndigenousHDR31). Another Indigenous HDR student mentioned the importance of speaking to other HDR students to learn from their experiences:

> Talk to every single PhD candidate you can about their experience in the school/institution they are in, where possible choose your supervisor with great care (erring on personal relationship if in doubt because that will help you in the long run) but realise that the HE sector is pretty fluid right now and the chances that you will have to change supervisor at some point is very high (they move jobs, have lives, etc.) (OLS2_IndigenousHDR19).

The need to understand how other HDR students were able to submit theses or dissertations was also recommended as a strategy that "speak to current PhD students about the struggles of PhD life. Speak to those students who have recently submitted about what it took to get across the line" (OLS2_IndigenousHDR23).

Having a support system that includes your supervisory team was also recommended:

> Make sure you pick a topic that is true to yourself and a supervisor who understands and respects your vision. Also, ensure you have a support system, because it can and will get very hard (OLS2_IndigenousHDR28).

The importance of reconnecting was also mentioned that "Take time each day to reconnect with country, family and our ancestors. Draw strength from them and remind yourself daily of why you are doing research" (OLS2_IndigenousHDR30).

From the above advice from Indigenous HDR students to prospective research student, it can be seen that there is a mix of both strategic advice relating to supervisors and completing the degree and well-being advice about ensuring you have support systems in place.

8.7 Summary

In this chapter, we have extended the recommendations for ensuring the success pathway of Indigenous HDR students. Our recommendations are applicable to decision-makers who are able to create positions for Indigenous HDR students to transition to academic positions during their research degrees, as well to supervisors and prospective HDR students. We hope the insights from Indigenous HDR students across Australia provide a glimpse into what is needed to make improvements that might result in more Indigenous HDR completions and more Indigenous academics in higher education institutions. We thank all the Indigenous HDR students who participated in our research projects and/or capacity-building workshop offered through National Indigenous Research and Knowledges Network (NIRAKN) over the years. We wish continued success to all Indigenous HDR around the globe.

Throughout this book and these research projects, good rapport between Indigenous HDR students and supervisors was highlighted to be a key enabling factor for Indigenous HDR students to succeed. Although the relationship between Indigenous

HDR students and supervisors is well addressed across this book, the role gender plays in the supervisory relationship was not explored. Identifying what role gender plays in the ongoing success of the Indigenous student–supervisor relationship is an area for further work.

References

Barnhardt, R. (2002). Domestication of the ivory tower: Institutional adaptation to cultural distance. *Anthropology & Education Quarterly, 33*(2), 238–249. https://doi.org/10.1525/aeq.2002.33.2.238
Hauser, V., Howlett, C., & Matthews, C. (2009). The place of Indigenous knowledge in tertiary science education: A case study of Canadian practices in indigenising the curriculum. *The Australian Journal of Indigenous Education, 38*(S1), 46–58. https://doi.org/10.1375/S1326011100000082X
McKinley, E., Grant, B., Middleton, S., Irwin, K., & Williams, L. R. T. (2011). Working at the interface: Indigenous students' experience of undertaking doctoral studies in Aotearoa New Zealand. *Equity & Excellence in Education, 44*(1), 115–132. https://doi.org/10.1080/10665684.2010.540972
Moreton-Robinson, A., Anderson, P., Blue, L. E., Nguyen, L., & Pham, T. (2020). *Report on Indigenous success in higher degree by research*. Prepared for the Australian Government, Department of Education and Training. https://www.qut.edu.au/?a=921040
Schmelkes, S. (2009). Intercultural universities in Mexico: Progress and difficulties. *Intercultural Education, 20*(1), 5–17. https://doi.org/10.1080/14675980802700649
Schofield, T., O'Brien, R., & Gilroy, J. (2013). Indigenous higher education: Overcoming barriers to participation in research higher degree programs. *Australian Aboriginal Studies, 2*, 13–28.
Trudgett, M. (2011). Western places, academic spaces and Indigenous faces: Supervising Indigenous Australian postgraduate students. *Teaching in Higher Education, 16*(4), 389–399. https://doi.org/10.1080/13562517.2011.560376
Wilson, M., Hunt, M., Richardson, L., Phillips, H., Richardson, K., & Challies, D. (2011). Āwhina: A programme for Māori and Pacific tertiary science graduate and postgraduate success. *Higher Education, 62*(6), 699–719. https://doi.org/10.1007/s10734-011-9413-3

Open Access This chapter is licensed under the terms of the Creative Commons Attribution 4.0 International License (http://creativecommons.org/licenses/by/4.0/), which permits use, sharing, adaptation, distribution and reproduction in any medium or format, as long as you give appropriate credit to the original author(s) and the source, provide a link to the Creative Commons license and indicate if changes were made.

The images or other third party material in this chapter are included in the chapter's Creative Commons license, unless indicated otherwise in a credit line to the material. If material is not included in the chapter's Creative Commons license and your intended use is not permitted by statutory regulation or exceeds the permitted use, you will need to obtain permission directly from the copyright holder.

The manufacturer's authorised representative in the EU is Springer Nature Customer Service Centre GmbH, Europaplatz 3, 69115 Heidelberg, Germany. If you have any concerns regarding our products, please contact ProductSafety@springernature.com

Printed and bound by CPI Group (UK) Ltd, Croydon, CR0 4YY

24/03/2026

02077373-0004